The Love Suicide at
Schofield Barracks
and
Democracy and Esther

Also by Romulus Linney

Heathen Valley
Slowly, by Thy Hand Unfurled
The Sorrows of Frederick

The Love Suicide at Schofield Barracks

Democracy and Esther

Two Plays by
ROMULUS LINNEY

HARCOURT BRACE JOVANOVICH, INC.
NEW YORK

First edition

ISBN 0–15–154725–4
Library of Congress Catalog Card Number: 72–91836

Printed in the United States of America
B C D E

For M.J.

Contents

Preface

This book contains two plays about American values, in the 1870's and in the 1970's. Each was first produced in the Off Broadway theatre of the HB Playwrights Foundation in New York, under the able direction of Herbert Berghof. *The Love Suicide at Schofield Barracks* subsequently received a grant from the American National Theatre and Academy and was produced on Broadway under the auspices of Cheryl Crawford and Konrad Matthaei.

Democracy and Esther is a dramatization of two nineteenth-century novels by Henry Adams, whose great grandfather was this nation's second President, whose grandfather was its sixth President, whose father was its Ambassador to Great Britain, and who in his turn became its keen, disillusioned critical historian. In all the works of Henry Adams, from the solid *History of the United States during the Administrations of Jefferson and Madison*, to the devastating and beautiful *Education of Henry Adams*, he refuses to be awed by the future of American power, or overly impressed by the American Dream. His loyal but open lack of faith in his country made him many enemies, but makes Henry Adams today a wise prophet of the enduring imperfections in our way of life.

He expressed his lack of faith most clearly in his novels: *Democracy*, published anonymously in 1880, and *Esther*, published in 1884, under the bland, delicious pseudonym of Francis Snow Compton. *Democracy*, a best seller, was considered at the time scandalous gossip of amorous corruption in Washington. *Esther*, beloved by Adams and ignored by the public, was an idealization of his wife, and a loving tribute to the warmth and honesty of a troubled personality. Both novels confront basic American dilemmas, magnified, it seems to me, by ninety years of American life. They are dramatized here into one play, their two stories combined. The result is a free adaptation for the stage, containing much dialogue and several situations of my own, but aiming to keep the spirit of Henry Adams's characters intact.

The Love Suicide at Schofield Barracks, an original play, extends conflicts of American idealism versus American pragmatism into the present. While Henry Adams's two heroines, idealized and symbolic, as women often were for him, painfully accept some harsh American realities, they are still able to choose the extent of their personal commitment—in this case, marriage. In *The Love Suicide at Schofield Barracks*, the same acceptance occurs, but now by two people as irrevocably wedded to their country and to each other as any I could imagine: a Major General in the United States Army and a devoted, patriotic wife. That experience would be no comedy. Their pain could be severe indeed, a disgrace, in fact, of ideals held closer than many ordinary citizens could imagine. Its only exorcism, I fancied, might be the only one there is, a Japanese ritual, often performed in that nation's literature and life. I set this oriental conception against American experience. The result is not a realistic condemnation of the Army, or a military satire, or a tract for universal peace. It is an old story, familiar in Japan, about converging irreconcilable convictions, a play about a man and his wife who chose to forsake one conviction for another, and about the effect their personal ritual of redemption had upon the Americans who witnessed it.

I would like to express here my gratitude to Herbert Berghof and the HB Playwrights Foundation for helpful encouragement while I worked on these plays.

The Love Suicide at
Schofield Barracks

War is a science, perhaps, but it depends
on art for its application.
                    —The Commanding General
                       of Schofield Barracks

I was caught by obligations from which I
could not withdraw.
                    —Chikamatsu Monzaemon
                       The Love Suicides at Amijima

CHARACTERS

CAPTAIN MARTIN
THE COMMANDING OFFICER
PRIVATE FIRST CLASS BOWERS
MASTER SERGEANT BATES
KATHERINE NOMURA
WARRANT OFFICER LEVANDRE
MAJOR CASSIDY
LIEUTENANT GENERAL EVANS
SERGEANT MAJOR RUGGLES
LUCY LAKE
COLONEL MOORE
MRS. NORVEL BATES
JUDITH BORDEN
A FRIEND
EDWARD ROUNDHOUSE
VOICES
TWO DANCERS

PLACE: The dance floor of the Officers' Club ballroom, Schofield Barracks, Hawaii

TIME: Just after Halloween, 1970

Prologue

———•◦•———

The inquiry was held on the ballroom dance floor of the Officers' Club, Schofield Barracks, Hawaii, where the event itself took place. It was conducted on Monday morning, November 2, 1970, by the new Commanding Officer of the division, Brigadier General Thomas N. Borden. General Borden was not present when the event took place. When informed by field telephone of what had happened, he ordered immediate autopsies and the ballroom sealed by Military Police. He then notified Pacific Army Headquarters and returned at once to Schofield Barracks.

The Officers' Club there is a pleasant, modest brick building, reminiscent of an American small-town country club. Its central, multipurpose room is used for various garrison-life meetings and conferences as well as for parties, banquets and dances, but it is called the ballroom because at one end of the room there is a small stage and bandstand and a circular wooden dance floor. The atmosphere is cheerfully functional, rather like a Holiday Inn.

The Commanding Officer arrived at 3:30 A.M., Sunday. He went at once to the Officers' Club and entered the ballroom alone. Confronting him were the remains of an Officers' Club Halloween party, left in the exact and terrific disorder in which it had ended. Outlandish cardboard witches, skeletons, skulls, comic-book ghosts and cut-out hobgoblins of all kinds were hanging from the ceiling and fixed to the walls. Overhead swept orange and black streamers, with paper cats, bats and spiders caught in their tangles. Around the dance floor itself, a circle of inlaid parquet, and on it, were overturned chairs, tables, stained tablecloths, cups, glasses and plates, many broken. Large pumpkins, with diamond-shaped eyes, jagged mouths and collapsed, burned-out foreheads grinned on tables still standing or lay on the floor. Bowls of nuts, already rotting fruit and yellow candy corn littered the room.

Facing the dance floor and the bandstand stage behind it were four extraordinary American antique Hepplewhite armchairs, with sturdy mahogany frames and richly woven brocade upholstery. The arms of these chairs, extended slightly, ended in small carved faces of eagles. All four chairs were marked with large and ostentatious signs saying RESERVED.

At the center of the dance floor, the Commanding Officer found two Japanese gowns, heavily bloodstained. He found two masks, from the classical Japanese Noh theatre, also bloody. He found an Army automatic 45-caliber pistol and a professional archer's hunting bow, with a bloodstained arrow lying several feet away. On the small bandstand stage, its white plastic glare shining against the scarlet stage curtain, he saw a portable infant's toilet. On the curtain, almost lost in the red velure texture, and splattered all the way down the steps from the stage leading onto the center of the dance floor were the remains of a human head, shattered, brains and skull exploded outward by some great force.

The Commanding Officer ordered the room opened, brightly lit by searchlights, and everything there photographed in great detail. He then ordered the room to be cleaned and set in order, but by his command the Halloween decorations were all retained and stacked against one wall.

The chairs marked RESERVED he left exactly where they were. He then provided a list of fifteen people, who were to be telephoned early Sunday morning. They were to be asked, with every courtesy and consideration, if they would come to an inquiry, which he would conduct at ten o'clock Monday morning. Then he telephoned Pacific Army Headquarters again, went to his quarters, and tried to sleep.

At ten o'clock Monday morning, twelve of the fifteen people called arrived at the Officers' Club. There they were greeted by Captain Terence X. Martin, a tactful and pleasant but efficient young Courts and Boards officer, from Urbana, Illinois.

Captain Martin led them into the ballroom, doing his best to make them as much at ease as possible. Comfortable chairs from the Club lobby had been placed around the dance floor, more or less where the officers, their wives and guests sat during the Halloween party. Captain Martin had made sure everyone had a table by his chair, and there were pitchers of ice water and glasses, cigarettes, matches and ashtrays on them. Reactions differed. Some could not look at the dance floor at all. Others searched, a few avidly, for human gore, now vanished. The wooden circle lay clean and spotless before them, a shining void, its polished surface gleaming in bright and cheerful morning light.

Captain Martin had prepared the room according to specifications from the Commanding Officer. Behind the dance floor was the stage, red curtains closed. To one side was a table for the use of the Commanding Officer, on it necessary papers, documents and a telephone. On a second, somewhat lower, table beside it lay objects the Commanding Officer had marked in evidence: the bow, the arrow, the pistol, the bloodstained gowns, the two Japanese theatre masks, and the infant's toilet, placed in a cardboard box.

7

Facing the dance floor, as before, sat the four American antique armchairs, their RESERVED signs intact. On the other side of the dance floor, removed from the Commanding Officer's table, there was a smaller table and chair for the use of Captain Martin, equipped with copies of the papers and documents, a telephone and a tape recorder.

At 10:15, the Commanding Officer entered the room. Politely, General Borden thanked all personnel, both military and civilian, for coming to this unusual inquiry, for which he frankly admitted he had no precedent whatsoever. He explained that it was not to be considered a military trial in any way, and was, in fact, not even the official inquest. And that it was their co-operation alone that made the inquiry possible at all. They would be asked questions, but each and every one of them was to feel absolutely free to answer or not, and, at the end of the questions, to present their own views of the matter and say anything they pleased. His only request was that if they agreed to participate, they would stay until the end of the inquiry, which would not take long, and would allow him use of their testimonies and opinions, which would be tape-recorded. He then sat at his table and studied his papers for a moment, giving anyone who wanted it a chance to leave the room. No one did. He told Captain Martin to begin the inquiry.

Act One

[CAPTAIN MARTIN *places a comfortable leather chair on swivels at the center of the dance floor. He turns on a small tape recorder.*]

CAPTAIN MARTIN: Private First Class Richard E. Bowers, please.

[PRIVATE BOWERS *steps forward. He is a young and intelligent draftee. He sits in the leather chair.*]

Private Bowers, this is a very informal inquiry. You may answer or not.

BOWERS: Yes, sir.

MARTIN: Will you describe your duties here on the night of October 31st?

BOWERS: Yes, sir. As Public Information Office reporter and photographer, I was to take pictures and write an account of the annual Post Halloween Party, and release it immediately to all news media. PIO had orders to that effect from the General's office.

MARTIN: And we all read the papers, Private. You certainly did your duty.

BOWERS: Thank you, sir.

MARTIN: Before the incident occurred, Private Bowers,

did you notice anything unusual about the preliminaries, or about the evening itself?

BOWERS [*wary*]: Well, I guess I did, yes, sir.

CO: Answer as you wish, Private. No one is on trial. And nobody blames you for releasing your story.

BOWERS: All right, sir. Yes, I certainly did notice unusual things. First of all, everybody stayed sober.

MARTIN: And you found that unusual?

BOWERS: I sure did.

MARTIN: Are you making remarks, Private, or testifying?

BOWERS: Testifying, sir. I know the difference.

MARTIN: Since it says here you are a Princeton graduate, let us hope so. Clarify that remark.

BOWERS: Certainly. I cover Officers' Club parties all the time. Drinks, appetizers, drinks, dinner, drinks, entertainment, drinks, dancing, drinks. By ten o'clock almost everybody is smashed, and they stay that way, or get worse. It has often occurred to me that military parties would make an excellent substitute for war itself.

MARTIN: Now, *that* was a remark!

BOWERS [*coolly*]: Yes, sir. I apologize. Shall I continue?

CO: With a warning from me. In spite of the lenient and informal nature of this proceeding, it is not going to be a college philosophy class. Proceed.

BOWERS: Yes, sir. But all I can truthfully say is, I watched a lot of drunks not getting drunk. Then the General came in drunk, and his wife was drunk with him. That, and what they had on, just blew everybody's mind.

MARTIN: Go to that table, Private. Are those the gowns they wore?

[BOWERS *goes to the table. The gowns and the masks are in boxes; we cannot see them. The other items are visible.* BOWERS *inspects the gowns.*]

BOWERS: Yes, sir. In they came, in these gowns, and wearing these masks. Some kind of oriental demon and a beautiful Japanese lady.

MARTIN: Then what happened?

BOWERS: They sat right here. They were separated from everybody else by two empty chairs, here, on each side of them, marked with big RESERVED signs. And they simply sat there, like oriental ghosts. Now and then they would tip the bottoms of their masks, and drink punch. I took a picture; then Major Cassidy grabbed me and said no more pictures tonight of anybody. But I did get that one. Would you like to see it?

CO: Please.

[MARTIN *starts to get the picture which* BOWERS *has with him in a Manila envelope, but* BOWERS *gets up, gives it to the* CO *himself. The* CO *stares at it, in amazement, then nods to* MARTIN.]

MARTIN: And then what happened, Private?

BOWERS: The festivities continued. Entertainment. Ballroom dancers from Waikiki. Some band numbers. A Lieutenant Colonel's wife gave everybody a demonstration of South Carolina birdcalls. A few awkward party games, on the dance floor, here. But all the time with those two foreign demons watching, and drinking.

[MARTIN *takes a carton of sound-recording tape from his desk and hands it to* BOWERS.]

MARTIN: Is this the tape you made?

BOWERS: Yes, sir. PIO had orders, from the General. The microphone sat right up there on the bandstand. It took all the entertainment down on tape. The whole thing was bugged, by the General. How do you think I got my story out so fast?

MARTIN: You transcribed what happened, is that right?

BOWERS: Yes, sir.

MARTIN: And did you bring us copies of that, Private?

BOWERS: As ordered. Yes, sir. [*He hands* MARTIN *several sets of typed pages, clipped together.*]

MARTIN: All right. Now then, was that all of the entertainment?

BOWERS: That was it. Until, of course, they took over everything themselves.

CO: Thank you, Private Bowers. Do you have anything you wish to add? Now is the time for your remarks, if you have any left.

BOWERS: I have just one, sir. I wish I was home.

MARTIN: All right, Private. Please remain in the room.

[BOWERS *steps down.*]

12

Master Sergeant Norvel T. Bates, please.

[*A well-worn NCO, in his forties, takes the stand.*]

Sergeant Bates, you understand this is a somewhat unusual board of inquiry. You are not required to answer under oath or against your wishes.

BATES: I understand, sir.

MARTIN: Good. You are on the General's office staff?

BATES: I am the General's Enlisted Aide.

MARTIN: And you've been assigned to him for some time? Several years, in fact?

BATES: Yes, sir.

MARTIN: Sergeant, we have a note here from the General recommending you very highly. Were you aware of his esteem?

BATES [*in sorrow*]: We knew each other pretty well.

MARTIN: You played a large part in the General's preparations. Can you describe it for us?

BATES: I'll do my best. Late Saturday morning, I was summoned to the General's quarters. He handed me a sealed Manila envelope. In it was a General Order he had written out by hand and signed, and then stenciled himself. I had clearance to process it. [*To the* CO] I did, and that is the order you received, sir, for this inquiry.

CO: Right. Go ahead, Sergeant.

BATES: After that, he asked me to sit down for a moment. He made me a drink. His wife joined us. They told me

13

they had just written a sort of play together. A play for two masks they'd found in Japan, when they were first married and starting a family, serving abroad. The masks meant a great deal to them, they said.

CO: What did you think about that?

BATES: I was certainly surprised they would be writing plays, but I tried to show polite interest. Then they asked me to help them.

CO: You mean be in the play?

BATES: Yes, sir. They asked me if I would read part of their play aloud, together with their private secretary, a Miss Nomura, at the Officers' Club Halloween party Saturday night.

CO: What did you think of their play?

BATES: I didn't understand it. I thought it was silly. When I saw one of the last lines said "I will wait for you in heaven, my noble husband," I thought, Oh Lord. But, sir, I can't tell you how much I admired the General and his wife. I respected them both, and everything they stood for. And if what they really wanted to do was make fools out of themselves at a party, then I was glad to be right there with them.

CO: What else were you asked to do?

BATES: On the porch, as I was leaving, the General gave me verbal instructions. He told me no matter what happened, I was to return to his quarters right after the party and take possession of papers I would find on a card table in the living room.

CO: And you did that?

BATES: Yes, sir. In shock, but I did it. With my wife, Lorna.

CO: And what were they?

BATES: First, the will. The General and his wife liquidated their estate. It was a lot of money, and they left it all to an Oriental-American orphanage. There is a certified check already in the mail, on its way to the orphanage now.

CO: How much was it?

BATES: Three hundred and fifty-five thousand dollars. They gave that orphanage everything they had.

CO: And what else did you find?

BATES: Stacks of all kinds of resignations, cancellations, from everything in the world. On top, his resignation from the American Archery Association and from the Army of the United States. And then—of course—

CO: Yes?

BATES: Their bodies.

CO: Explain.

BATES: Notarized document, donating their bodies to a civilian research hospital in Honolulu.

CO: Thank you, Sergeant. Anything else?

BATES: Yes, sir. This envelope, sealed. It says on the front that I am to open it and read the contents to you at the end of this inquiry, if, as the General directed, you conduct it. If not, I'm to destroy it. His signature is on it, here.

CO: Let me see that, please. [*He looks at the envelope a moment, then briskly hands it back to* BATES.] And that's what you'll do, Sergeant. As directed.

BATES: Yes, sir.

CO: Thank you very much. Is there anything else you, yourself, wish to add?

BATES: Yes, sir. I agree with Private Bowers. For the first time in seventeen years with the Army, I wish to God I was home.

MARTIN: Thank you. Please remain in the room, Sergeant. Miss Katherine Nomura, please.

[*A young Japanese-American woman takes the stand.*]

Miss Nomura, this is a very informal inquiry. You may answer or not, as you see fit, and we are much obliged for your help. Do you understand?

MISS NOMURA: Oh, yes.

MARTIN: How long have you been in the service of the General?

MISS NOMURA: Four days.

MARTIN: How did you come to work for him?

MISS NOMURA: I was sent to him from a commercial bureau. I fitted all his requirements.

MARTIN: And what were your duties?

MISS NOMURA: Very light secretarial work, for his wife. I know now, of course, it was to read the play. Which also explains his requirements.

MARTIN: What were they?

MISS NOMURA: They were for a female with a fondness for oriental theatre and knowledge of it. Who should be Japanese, and who should have one other qualification I prefer not to mention. He had some trouble finding me.

MARTIN: I see. And you read part of the play aloud, with Sergeant Bates, on Saturday night?

MISS NOMURA: Yes.

MARTIN: What did you think of it?

MISS NOMURA: I thought it very beautiful.

MARTIN: Why?

MISS NOMURA: I knew what it was they had written. It is an old Japanese story.

MARTIN: What is?

MISS NOMURA: Their play. It is a *shinju*.

MARTIN: And what is that?

MISS NOMURA: A love suicide. A kind of play in which lovers, who cannot bear the cruelty of the world, commit suicide together. There have been a great many of them.

MARTIN: Do you mean plays, or love suicides?

MISS NOMURA: Both.

MARTIN: I see. Now, Miss Nomura—

MISS NOMURA: Please. One other thing. It is not a sin, or a disgrace. It is release from illusion, and embrace of

17

eternal truth. Their life becomes a beautiful poem they leave behind, and is considered a great achievement. They are taken directly into heaven and are reborn on lotus leaves. Thank you.

MARTIN: Thank you. Now, Miss Nomura—

CO [*breaking in*]: Miss Nomura, did you therefore have any idea of the actual purpose of this play?

MISS NOMURA: Oh, yes.

CO: You did?

MISS NOMURA: I said yes.

CO: You mean you knew Saturday night they were going to kill themselves on this dance floor?

MISS NOMURA: I knew they were going to act out a *shinju* on this dance floor. It also occurred to me that they might be in earnest.

CO: Then, pardon me, Miss Nomura, but why didn't you tell anyone?

MISS NOMURA: That would have spoiled a *shinju*. A sacred act. [*Smiling*] Besides, who would have believed me? Would you? And would you have asked the Commanding General, at a party, if he intended to kill himself that evening?

CO: I see what you mean. What else did they tell you about the performance they had planned?

MISS NOMURA: Nothing. I was to meet with Sergeant Bates at the Officers' Club at about ten o'clock. We were to read our parts aloud, while they acted out their play on the dance floor.

CO: And you knew what they might really do?

MISS NOMURA: I said yes. [*Pause*] If a man and his wife discover their home is ugly and wish to find a better one, is that a cause for alarm?

CO: Thank you very much, Miss Nomura. I'm sure I don't know. Is there anything you wish to add?

MISS NOMURA: Oh, yes. I am glad I saw what I saw. [*She steps down.*]

MARTIN: Sir, next on our list is Major Cassidy, ranking medical officer at the party Saturday night. He's held up at the dispensary and will be here as soon as he can.

CO: All right. Call him when he gets here. Go on to the next one.

MARTIN: Mr. Edward Roundhouse, please.

[*No response*]

Mr. Edward Roundhouse?

[*No response*]

Sir, Mr. Roundhouse is not present.

CO: Who is he?

MARTIN: He owns a restaurant on the windward side of the island, sir. It's called "The Breeze and I." Very popular as a tourist stop.

CO: Charming. Proceed.

MARTIN: Yes, sir. Warrant Officer Morton R. Le-vaun-dre, please.

[*An unsoldierly looking soldier, highly emotional in nature, steps up.*]

LEVANDRE: Le*van*der. Pronounced Le-*van-der*.

MARTIN: I see. Mr. Levandre, you may answer or not. And add whatever you please.

LEVANDRE: Very well.

MARTIN: You are the director of the division band?

LEVANDRE: Yes.

MARTIN: And, as a published composer, you were musical consultant for the division?

LEVANDRE: I still am.

MARTIN: Mr. Levandre, were you here at the party Saturday night?

LEVANDRE: I was not. Thank goodness.

MARTIN: I see. A short time ago, the General called you in. Correct?

LEVANDRE: Yes.

MARTIN: What did he want?

LEVANDRE: He wanted to know the name of an opera. He described the plot; it was *Tristan und Isolde.* "All right," he said, and he sent me downtown with a jeep and a driver to get recordings of it. By the time we got back to Schofield, it was late, getting dark. The driver wouldn't take me to my barracks. Orders, he said. And he left me there!

MARTIN: Where?

LEVANDRE: Why, out by that gigantic ugly old Signal Corps warehouse, at the far end of the post. He was in there all by himself.

MARTIN: What were you supposed to do?

LEVANDRE: Play the records for him. He had the Signal Corps set up speakers all over the warehouse. So we played the whole last act of *Tristan und Isolde*. There we were. Me and a major general. And Wagner. And Tristan. And Isolde. All of us in there together.

MARTIN: All right. You both listened to the end of the opera.

LEVANDRE: Twice. Once just for him to hear it again, and once more after I had received my commission.

MARTIN: And what was that?

LEVANDRE: To write him a *Liebestod*.

MARTIN: A what?

LEVANDRE: A Liebestod. A Love-Death. Like Richard Wagner's. Where great lovers die in fire together.

CO: He asked you *that?*

LEVANDRE: Yes, sir. He sure did. And I felt—well—just—

CO: Say what you want to say.

LEVANDRE: That he was stupid! Insulting me! I got very angry!

CO: Why?

LEVANDRE: To be asked to do such a thing! *Tristan!* I just compose band pieces and brass ensemble things. I am

21

the sort of person who got hold of the tuba, you know, as a boy, and did the French horn in high school. Music major in college. Graduate work, state university. Someday, I hope to teach school myself, in some college music department, somewhere small, in some little town. Where music is—kind. Exciting, yes, but decent, too. Well, I didn't like what he was doing!

CO: What do you mean?

LEVANDRE: Listening to Wagner like that. Walking around that enormous warehouse thinking God knows what. Once, he stopped, right at some terrific climax in the music, and stared out the window. He threw it open, suddenly, with great force, and pointed out. He was very emphatic! I jumped three feet. "Look," he said. "Look at that mountain. The last rays of the sun. Red, and gold, and now turning black, like a mountain in hell." I said, "Yes, sir!" And Wagner screamed love-death all over the place.

CO: And what did you do?

LEVANDRE: He was the Commanding General: I got a *Liebestod* for him. I telegraphed a friend back in Boston, a real composer, and asked him for God's sake get me out of this. Few days later, I got a tape in the mail. He had put the *Liebestod* through a Moog Synthesizer, and wrote: "Give that to the General, and tell him to shove it; Wagner's dead."

CO: And did you tell the General that?

LEVANDRE: Well, no. But when I played the tape, he liked it. "Modern, isn't it?" he said. I said, "Yes, sir, it is." And that was that. Until, of course, I heard he'd used it for that horrible thing he did to himself at the Halloween party. Then I knew what he had been doing with me.

CO: Thank you. Do you have anything you wish to add? The General himself specified everyone be asked this. His own directive gives you complete freedom to express yourself.

LEVANDRE: Yes, sir, I do want to say something. I resent what he did to me very much. I'm sorry the man's dead, but that frankly doesn't change my feelings.

CO: What do you resent?

LEVANDRE: Myself, and music, being used like that. I'm a soldier, too. I don't mind direct orders. I've stayed in the Army because I don't mind direct orders. But I do mind being used. Between serving and being used there's a *difference*, a *distinction*—and by a man like that! He was a fool! No wonder he liked Wagner.

CO: Don't you like Wagner?

LEVANDRE: Yes, sir. I love Wagner. On the *stage*, sung by tenors and sopranos: big, fat, silly, harmless opera stars! Then the music is sublime, of course. But not when you hear it like that, like he did: serious, arrogant and ignorant. And decide to use it.

CO: I see your point.

LEVANDRE: But—

CO: Yes?

LEVANDRE: He was polite to me. And considerate. Even grateful. He—well, put his arm around my shoulders, when I gave him the tape. I didn't dislike him person-ally. I just—well, I don't know. I'm sorry. [*He steps down.*]

[MAJOR CASSIDY *has entered, and is called imme-diately.*]

MARTIN: Major Richard C. Cassidy, please.

[MAJOR CASSIDY *takes the witness chair.*]

Sir, you were at the Club on the night of October 31st?

CASSIDY: Yes.

MARTIN: Major, as the General's physician, did you have any prior knowledge of the extreme action he meant to take?

CASSIDY: I had—not knowledge of it, no—but—

CO: Take your time, Major.

CASSIDY: Sir, may I just tell you what happened between us? Will that do?

CO: Of course.

CASSIDY: Thursday morning, the General slipped, climb-ing out of a mortar entrenchment. He cut his scalp on a gun wheel, not seriously, but scalp wounds bleed freely, and that upset him. I gave him a sedative and fixed him up. No stitches, or clamps. But while I did that, he said some—well, alarming things. They made no sense but they were alarming.

CO: What were they?

CASSIDY [*very uncertain*]: Sir, I am not at all sure I should answer.

CO: Suit yourself. It's your decision, Major.

CASSIDY: Well, he said he was going to heaven, where he would stop the war.

CO [*sharply*]: *What?*

CASSIDY: He said he was going to die, but in such a way that when he appeared in heaven, God would stop the war. Now, you can believe me or not.

CO: You mean he was delirious, is that what you're saying?

CASSIDY: Well, of course.

CO: All right, Major. How long was he in this state of mind?

CASSIDY: Not long.

CO: Go on.

CASSIDY: That was all, until the party. We were all there waiting for the General and his wife to come to dinner, which they never did. So we all had dinner without them. And then, God help us, the man and his wife came walking in here on us at 10:30, wearing those damned crazy gowns and masks!

CO: Now, Major, didn't you feel the man might be mentally—

CASSIDY: No, sir! We all knew the General. He simply wasn't the sort of man you would think that about.

CO: I might if he'd told me he was going to heaven to stop a war. Didn't you even make a report on that, Major?

CASSIDY: Sir, that business in the dispensary was just a flash. A vision, under blood shock and sedation. Happens to people all the time. That doesn't mean there was any question of the General's competence, or any interference with him on my part whatsoever.

CO: Not even during the play?

CASSIDY: Well, there you have me. And every other person who sat here around this dance floor. I suppose—we might have stopped it, but we didn't. We just didn't.

CO: Frankly, I find that hard to believe.

CASSIDY: Sir, you didn't see the play.

CO: But I have seen your medical report, Major. And I find it confused, to say the least. You report her death a suicide. Why? [*Pointing to the bow on the table*] He *shot* her with that thing, didn't he? That is murder, isn't it?

CASSIDY: Both deaths were suicide.

CO: I find that preposterous. It was a murder and *then* a suicide!

CASSIDY: You didn't see the play.

[*A pause*]

CO: So I didn't. All right, Major, read your report. I'll try again.

CASSIDY: Yes, sir. [*He takes it from an envelope.*]

[*The telephone on* CAPTAIN MARTIN's *desk rings. He answers it, whispering, sets it down quickly, moves swiftly to the* CO *and whispers to him, in some confusion.*]

CO [*To* MARTIN]: Well, God, yes, go get him.

[MARTIN *goes, quickly.*]

[*To* CASSIDY] Major, we will interrupt your testimony. Step down and stand by. Thank you.

[CASSIDY *steps down. Visibly shaken,* MARTIN *comes back in swiftly.*]

MARTIN: Sir, Lieutenant General Evans.

[*The* CO *stands up quickly.* GENERAL EVANS, *a three-star general in the American Army, enters. He is no caricature of an Army officer, but a formidable, highly intelligent, very individual man in his fifties. There is perhaps more force to him than polish, but there is polish, too, and sensitivity, and great natural dignity. He enters slowly, looking about at everyone, astonished that an inquiry is going on.*]

EVANS: General, I just got off the plane at Hickam Field. With orders to conduct an investigation of this tragedy. Orders from the United States Army Chief of Staff. Didn't you know I was coming?

CO: Yes, sir. I did.

EVANS: Then what in the world is this?

CO: The investigation, sir.

EVANS: That I am supposed to conduct?

CO: Yes, sir.

EVANS: And, as commanding officer, you are responsible, you gave the order. Correct?

CO: Yes, sir, and no, sir.

EVANS: *I beg your pardon?*

CO: Sir, while I am responsible for conducting this inquiry, I did not order it.

EVANS: Well, then, who did?

CO: Sir, the General himself.

EVANS [*stunned*]: What? *Mike?*

CO: Before he died, the General issued a direct order for this inquiry. To be held this morning. Openly, informally, with civilians present, and conducted by his own Executive Officer and new Commanding General of Schofield Barracks. Me.

EVANS: And that's what you've done?

CO: Yes, sir.

EVANS: Without consulting *anyone* at Army Headquarters? Letting *nobody* advise you in any way?

CO: That was part of the General's order.

EVANS: Carrying it out can put you in a hell of a spot.

CO: It already has. But his command was issued on Saturday afternoon, when he was still alive, in a United States Army General Order. It is absolutely legitimate; it constitutes my clear duty. It is my decision to accept the responsibility, and to follow his directive to the letter.

EVANS: Mike set this up?

CO: It is his own documentation of what happened to him. In the notes he left us, he mentions you. He says he sent for you. He hoped you would come, and he asks for your help.

28

EVANS [*with a deep sigh*]: Yes. Telegram, Saturday. It said: DON'T LET THEM SEND ANYONE BUT YOU SCHOFIELD MONDAY MORNING CRUCIAL GOOD-BY MIKE. I am here at my own request. The Chief of Staff approved it.

CO: Yes, sir.

EVANS: But you understand I must evaluate your inquiry, and you. I get on that plane with it tonight. You still assume responsibility?

CO: Yes, sir.

EVANS: All right, General. I'll help you any way I can. You're in command. Continue, as you think best.

CO: As Mike thought best.

EVANS: Agreed. Whether it finally is or not.

CO: Agreed.

EVANS: What do you want me to do?

CO: Sir, the General and I both ask you to be a witness.

EVANS: Okay. [*He takes the witness chair.*]

CO: Sir, you knew him personally for a long time?

EVANS: Thirty years. He was one of the finest general officers this miserable Army ever had. [*He takes a deep breath.*] Ah, what a shame! [*Pause*] I am so sorry he's gone! [*Crisply*] It is a great loss for his country, which he loved and defended.

CO: We will all agree to that.

[*A pause*]

29

EVANS: What? I'm all right! Fire away.

CO [*gently*]: You knew him well?

EVANS: Better than anyone. Except Sheila. When Avis and I were married, they were there. I was godfather to his son. And he, not long afterward, to mine. Wonderful people. Go on, General.

CO: Had you noticed anything different about him recently? Anything that might shed some light on this inquiry?

EVANS: No! Nothing! Now, we were realistic about the difficulties we're all in. Mike did not falter. He did his duty. He may have questioned it, but he did it! More than some, who don't question it, and don't do it! Damn it, he loved the Army. To answer your question: no. No.

[*A pause*]

CO: Yes, sir? Is there something you wish—

EVANS: Well, the boy.

CO: You mean his son?

EVANS: And mine. Among the many bonds holding us to-gether was the loss of both boys we were father and godfather to. I had a son killed in action. Mike gave me his silver star for my boy's memory, and, by God, not a year later I did the same for him! They all think back home that they are the only ones who lose their children to the war. We lost two boys that way! [*Pause*] Excuse me.

CO: I understand, sir.

EVANS: Maybe you do, and maybe you don't. Go on.

co: Well, there's just this. The question, in his own words, to ask you if you came here: "Have you recently noticed any change, intellectual or emotional, that might fore-shadow my public suicide?" His words.

[*A very long pause*]

EVANS: None! None! Mike! [*Pause*] I last saw him in July. He was called to Washington to give his opinion on certain antistatic field maneuvers on which he was a combat authority. We had lunch together. No sign of this! Of course, we both—

co: Yes, sir?

EVANS: Talked very specially, personally. We see each other mainly now to do that. We don't expect anyone else to understand.

co: Understand what, General?

EVANS: What it feels like to be proud of the useless sacrifice of your child.

co: Thank you. At this lunch, were there any other topics that might be—relevant to this inquiry?

EVANS: Military reform. We were both involved. Mike talked a lot about a new Code of Military Justice. We've got to have it, he said. Otherwise—[*Pause*]

co: Yes, General?

EVANS: They will laugh at us. Laughter, drugs and field officers shot in the back. And we will lose everything. [*Pause*] What? What was the question?

co: Relevant topics at lunch.

31

EVANS: No. Nothing else.

[MAJOR CASSIDY *looks at his watch, and slips out quietly, leaving his medical report on* MARTIN's *desk.*]

CO: One more thing, General. Which puzzles us all.

EVANS: Yes?

CO: A change of subject. Had the General and his wife ever taken much interest before in—ah—theatricals, or things of that nature? None of us here ever thought so.

EVANS: Well, now, let me see. [*Smiling*] Mike and Sheila and Avis and I were all in a Fort Ord production of *South Pacific*, back there in the fifties. Sheila used to sing in a club skit or two, and I guess Mike was Santa Claus once or twice. But that's all. I have no idea how they got involved in this terrible—[*Long pause*] Now, wait a minute.

CO: Yes, sir?

EVANS: Lunch again. I completely forgot. Mike insisted on bringing it up again.

CO: Yes, General?

EVANS [*remembering*]: It was a long time ago—1949. We were both stationed in Washington then. Mike had some kind of temporary liaison duty at Bethesda Naval Hospital. If you recall, James Forrestal, country's first Secretary of Defense, had just resigned his office. A fine man.

CO: I do recall. He was.

EVANS: The circumstances were peculiar. He had a nervous breakdown. They put him in Bethesda Naval Hospital.

His room was way up, nine or ten stories, and one night he went out an open window. Now, Mike was there on duty. He saw the open window, and the man's bed, with a book on it, open. [*Pause*] Now let me get this straight. Mike said it was open to a translation of one of those God-damned bloody Greek poems you read in school. There was a pen and paper there, too. Secretary Forrestal had been copying this thing out by hand, when he —well—jumped.

CO: Can you remember—

EVANS: Oh, yes. [*Smiling*] Mike made me remember. At lunch, after over twenty years. I didn't until he said, "Come on, now. I'll give you a hint. *Foaming Cleanser.*" I said, "What? Oh, come on!" Mike was like that; he could be whimsical about very serious things. But then I did get it, and I said, "All right. Ajax, the Foaming Cleanser," and he said, "Right."

CO: Foaming Cleanser, General?

EVANS: Right. The poem was from a play about Ajax, who was a Greek general, in the Trojan War. Mike told me what he'd found out about it. Ajax, it seems, toward the end of *that* mess, got bitter about something. Medals, status, something like that. So he decided he would get up in the middle of the night and kill all the other generals in their tents. Now—wait a minute—he did get to their tents, but then some goddess or other, of common sense or reason or something—

CO: Athena.

EVANS: That's right. She put a hex on him. Sent him instead into a big flock of sheep, where he just butchered

33

them. He dragged all the remains back into his tent, where he fell asleep thinking he had killed all his great enemies. When he woke up, the hex was gone. He found himself lying there in the guts and gore of dead innocent sheep, and when he finally realized what he'd done, he died of shame. Ran on his own sword. Mike said that was the passage Secretary Forrestal was copying by hand when he went out that hospital window. Now, whether or not it was a deep personal tragedy, or if Forrestal was also thinking about Ajax himself and what happened to him, and his country, is what Mike kept wondering about, and couldn't forget. Even after twenty years. Aside from that, it was all *South Pacific* and Santa Claus.

CO: Thank you, General. Is there anything you would like to add?

EVANS: Yes, there is. Mike was a wonderful general officer, but like the best men anywhere, like Forrestal, he did have odd, original streaks in him. Now, I don't know why he and Sheila did this terrible thing. Nobody could know them that well. But I do know it was a personal tragedy, like Forrestal's, and not a national one, or any kind of nonsense like that. Mike loved the Army, and the dignity of his service. What he did hasn't got one damn thing to do with lives we give and will always give for our country! All the lives! Nothing! Anything else?

CO: No, sir. Thank—

EVANS: Thank you. And proceed. [*He steps down.*]

[*The* CO *stands and waits until* GENERAL EVANS *takes a seat with him overlooking the inquiry.*]

34

CO [*to* MARTIN]: Recall Major Cassidy.

MARTIN: Sir, Major Cassidy is in surgery. He left his report here. Shall I read it for him?

CO: No, I want it from him. Get him back here before we finish. Go on to the next one.

MARTIN: Well, sir, next is Captain Harold D. Stretch, Company Commander, D Company, 18th Brigade. He's on sick call. Saturday night, he tried to make a joke out of everything. With this. [*He holds up the child's toilet.*]

EVANS: What the hell kind of man is Captain Stretch?

CO: Sir, he's never been promoted beyond company commander, and last month he was passed over for the last time. Saturday night, I suppose he didn't much care what he did, and so he played his joke on the General.

MARTIN: He's in the hospital now, with a temperature of a hundred and five.

CO: Well, let him stay there. Who's next?

MARTIN: Sergeant Major Reuben H. Ruggles, please.

[*A calm, cold-eyed, very professional soldier in his forties takes the stand. He carries a handsome swagger stick.*]

Sergeant Major Ruggles, do you understand the informal nature of these proceedings? That you don't have to answer a question if you don't want to?

RUGGLES [*quietly*]: I do, sir.

MARTIN [*with respect*]: I thought you would. His directive

characterizes you as the most effective noncommissioned officer the General has ever met.

CO: And I think we will all agree with that.

RUGGLES: I thank you, sir.

MARTIN: So what we would like to know, Sergeant Major, is your personal opinion of the General.

RUGGLES: Yes, sir. I prefer not to tell you.

MARTIN [*surprised*]: I see. Well, you had a consultation with him last week, is that right?

[RUGGLES *nods*.]

Can you tell us about that?

RUGGLES: To some degree, Lieutenant, sir. A private, D Company, 19th Infantry Brigade, a black man, had a nervous breakdown on the rifle range Friday morning. Live rounds; it was dangerous. But he was disarmed by a big Georgia Sergeant with a big red neck, who fractured the black man's skull. There was going to be some real trouble. The General took action.

MARTIN: What did he do?

RUGGLES: Several ineffective things. Then he consulted me.

MARTIN: And what did you do?

RUGGLES: I figured the race riot, or whatever was going to happen, was going to happen on Saturday, the next morning, at the big full Division parade. It had to. The General sent black cadre around Friday night and posted all his bulletins. Saturday morning, at the parade, we'd see. Now in two months, a black Sergeant,

12th Artillery, after his twenty years, was supposed to get out. Slated for a little parade. Two horns and a drum inside a quadrangle, where some Major would shake his hand that would be that. So on Friday night, I had a chat with a Personnel Specialist and then with our black Artillery Sergeant. I told him he was going to retire the next morning. He really didn't want to retire the next morning, but I convinced him.

MARTIN [*puzzled*]: Of what?

RUGGLES: To go home when he was told. Saturday morning, this Division massed for parade. Band started, flags unfurled, and when seven thousand combat-ready troops thundered past the reviewing stand, with tanks and artillery and choppers whirling in the air, wind, flags, the great Army in its glory, well—who do you think was standing up there to receive all those salutes? Just two men. The General and his black Sergeant, honored on the day of his retirement, whose name, by the way, believe it or not, is Remus. That's right. Reginald O. Remus. Well, everybody saluted the colors, and the colors saluted everybody, and it was all one big happy family. [*He laughs.*]

MARTIN [*revolted*]: In other words, what you did was put a nigger in the window, Sergeant Major, is that right?

[RUGGLES *stops laughing, looks mildly, dangerously, at* MARTIN.]

RUGGLES: You ought not to talk to me like that, son, sir. I am nearing the end of a long and honorable career. *I have done the state some service, and they know it.* That there's from Shakespeare. Watch out.

MARTIN [*coldly*]: After the parade, the General had a talk with you. What did you say to each other? If you please.

[*Ignoring* MARTIN *contemptuously,* RUGGLES *speaks directly to the* CO.]

RUGGLES: General, sir, what do I have to do here? Six weeks before *I* retire! I am only an enlisted man. I respectfully ask you to direct me.

CO: Follow your conscience, and say what you please. Whatever you say will be to your credit.

RUGGLES [*after a pause*]: Yeah. Thank you, sir. If that's what you want.

CO: That's what we want.

RUGGLES: After the parade, he took me in his office, closed the door, pulled out a bottle of Jack Daniel's. And we had a drink together.

[*A pause*]

MARTIN: And was that all?

RUGGLES: No, it wasn't all. He thanked me for the saving of his ass. Because putting Remus up there with him probably stopped a race riot, and certainly saved his ass. He was grateful, or something. Anyway, wanted to talk. Like we was chums.

MARTIN: What did he say?

RUGGLES: Lot of dumb things nobody knows the answer to. If I really thought the new all-professional Army could become a black dumping ground. Concerned, you know.

MARTIN: What did you say?

RUGGLES: I said I didn't know. What else? But I reckoned a mostly black army would have mostly black officers and mostly black parades, like in Haiti. He didn't like that idea, and changed the subject.

MARTIN: To what?

RUGGLES: Remus. Asked me if I knew why old Sergeant Remus kept his name. Why he never changed it. "Maybe he liked it," I said. "Remus ain't just a slave name. He was one of the founders of Rome. Didn't you know that, General?" "I guess I did, but I forgot," he he said. "What happened to Remus?" "Got killed," I said, "founding Rome. But she gave him his name, and he kept it, and so did Sergeant Remus, and so have I. We all made our deal with Rome, and we keep it for twenty years, and Rome keeps it for twenty years, and then we both got it made." "I don't understand," he said. "Well, General," I said, "maybe that's because you're not a Roman, really, and Remus is. And I am. I found that out in Korea. If you didn't, then I pity you."

EVANS [interrupting]: Sergeant Major, you spoke that way to your Commanding General?

RUGGLES: Why not, sir? *I'd just saved his damned ass for him, hadn't I?* One chance in twenty years to really talk to a general? Shit, I let go.

CO: All right. How?

RUGGLES: "Korea?" he said, politely, as if remembering the country was all I'd meant. "Yes, sir," I said. "Korea. When you and me was young, General, and made our bargains with Rome." "I don't know what your bargain was, Sergeant," he said, "but mine was to serve my country." "Mine was to kill," I said. "To kill what I was told to kill, and do it so well, my country would serve me." He didn't like that idea, either, and changed the subject again.

CO [*tersely*]: To?

RUGGLES: Nostalgia. He thought that would be safe. "What I remember," he said, "is fine long lines of marching men, and ice-cold night, starry freezing Korean skies, and the hard, lonely beauty of serving your country." "Well, what I remember," I said, "is a greenhorn country boy learning to kill. Scared to at first. Started learning on them wild dogs what couldn't stay away from our garbage, so we shot them. Then them Korean children. "*What?*" he said. "Children? What children?" "Oh, come on, General," I said. "You knowed the games played with them little rats. Don't tell me you didn't. Why, hell, you know who used to hand them live grenades, and bet which one would pull out the pin. I remember a country boy who got it down pat, learning to tell which fool kid would pull it first." "I never heard of anything like that!" he said. "Who was that?" "A damn good Roman soldier," I said. "Who went on to start killing the enemy, too. Why not? When he did that, you decorated him for it, and never asked what else he'd done. You never asked me, you never asked Remus. Oh, General, white men, black men, Rome gives us all our names. Then murders us, if it can. But if we survive, we keep our name, and are honorably retired with it. Fair enough, I said, twenty years ago, and so did old Remus. And we kept our bargain, and so did Rome. Except it wasn't to die for it, it was to kill for it, and live, to an honorable old age. I understand, I said, what a real soldier is, and I would rather have the common virtue of a killer than the glory of a fake like you." [*Pauses, stands*] And that was the end of the interview. Well, sir?

CO: All right, Sergeant Major. Anything else you want to say?

RUGGLES: As a matter of fact, sir, there is. When the General took over this Division, he gave me and the two other Sergeant Majors a swagger stick—this one here. He said he wasn't the smartest man in the world, but he was smart enough to know who really understood the Army: old-time regimental Sergeant Majors. He was always going to depend on us to tell him the truth, when his officers lied to him. That's exactly what I did. But my truth, it seems—since the man just shot himself —turned out stronger than his.

CO: All right. That's all. Please remain in the room.

RUGGLES: Thank you, sir. But I prefer not to. [*He walks deliberately out of the room and is gone.*]

[*The* CO *stares after him and then snaps back to* MARTIN.]

CO: Next!

MARTIN: Sir, I believe Lucy Lake came in just a moment ago. Should we call her now?

CO: Absolutely, if she's here.

MARTIN: Lucy Lake, please.

[*An extremely plain, blunt, white-haired, down-to-earth old New England woman takes the stand.*]

CO [*with charm and courtesy, truly impressed*]: Miss Lake, in his directive, the General tenders you an apology for taking up more of your valuable time. And speaking for the rest of us, allow me to thank you very much for coming here today.

LUCY LAKE: All right.

CO: We're all honored. Poets are not usually close friends with Generals. Am I right about that?

LUCY LAKE: No. I knew Archie Wavell in World War II very well. He loved poets.

CO: A British general, I believe. In America, however?

LUCY LAKE: America however, nope. Rare.

CO: You understand, Miss Lake, the somewhat peculiar nature of these proceedings?

LUCY LAKE: I get the idea.

CO: Good. How did you come to meet the General?

LUCY LAKE: I didn't. He came to meet me.

CO: When was that?

LUCY LAKE: Last summer.

CO: Can you tell us about this meeting, please?

LUCY LAKE: Breadloaf Conference, Middlebury, Vermont. Writers meet would-be writers, who pay to come, listen, and have their material read.

EVANS [*surprised, breaking in*]: Mike had been writing poetry?

LUCY LAKE: Yep.

EVANS: And he went there on his leave? His vacation?

LUCY LAKE: Yep.

EVANS: Go on.

LUCY LAKE: That's it. John Ciardi and I were working with the poets. We all met.

CO: What was your opinion of the General's poetry?

LUCY LAKE: Not just his. His wife's, too.

CO: *Their* poetry, then. What did you and Mr. Ciardi think of it?

LUCY LAKE: Oh, they were dilettantes, but not impossible. Bad, but not always completely. But, poets, you see, love very specific things, the concrete particulars of life, while Generals are—well, general. You could see that wrong with him. He didn't understand it at first, but he learned. And he did have a feeling for building, making a poem. Bringing disparate elements together. Yet I felt it was his wife who was truly remarkable.

EVANS: As a person, or a poet?

LUCY LAKE: Both. Poets are people, General, even when they may seem at times as mysterious to you as generals do to me. She was a lovely woman, sprightly, with a sharp eye. It was my pleasure to know her.

CO: Did they do or say anything unusual at this writers' conference?

LUCY LAKE: No. He was quite self-conscious. Said he was retired. They seldom came to the parties, with everybody else. Worked on their things. Took long walks.

Looked at Vermont, the mountains and the stars. They had a quiet, enriching cultural experience, just like it says in the brochure.

co: How about you, may I ask?

LUCY LAKE: Oh, I was drunk most of the time. It's a fun two weeks.

co: I see. When did you hear from them again?

LUCY LAKE: Just a month ago. Three lectures on American poetry, University of Hawaii. Money. I was in the newspaper, and General called. So I spent the last two weeks with them, in a little beach cottage they'd rented for me. Patrons, almost. Too bad they're dead.

co: Then, Miss Lake, you have actually been seeing both of them regularly for the past two weeks?

LUCY LAKE: Yep.

co: Well?

LUCY LAKE: Well?

co: Miss Lake, the General and his wife committed suicide Saturday night!

LUCY LAKE: I know it.

co: Well, haven't you any—didn't you notice—

LUCY LAKE: I noticed a lot. Some of it I may tell you about, and some of it I may not. You ask the questions, and I'll make up my mind as we go along.

co: Certainly. But my first question is this: You are really quite hostile to everything here, aren't you?

LUCY LAKE: Yep.

CO: Understood. In your meetings and conversations with the General and his wife, did they ever indicate anything unusual about themselves?

LUCY LAKE: General, you are going to have to be more specific.

CO: I'll do my best. Did they talk about suicide?

LUCY LAKE: Nope.

CO: Criticize the Army? The country?

LUCY LAKE: Never.

CO: Did they exhibit psychological peculiarities? Show nervous strain? Act or think in strange ways?

LUCY LAKE: No. I did all that. They were just fine, always quite composed. We simply talked about poetry and watched the sea. They drank a little, and I exhibited psychological peculiarities.

CO: I see.

LUCY LAKE: Good.

CO: But, Miss Lake, didn't anything about the General suggest anything at all—especially to a person as sensitive as you—about their evident deep despair, and their suicide?

LUCY LAKE: Nope.

CO [*angrily*]: Well, perhaps the man was trying, Miss Lake, and you were too drunk to pay him any attention! Is *that* a possibility?

[*A long pause*]

LUCY LAKE: They talked a lot about poetic drama. They wanted to write one. I told them, forget it, hardest thing to do there is. But they were both set on it, so I gave them some things to look up. Now, they had seen plenty of oriental theatre, but they'd never read Chikamatsu, eighteenth-century Jap playwright, who is really good. They were crazy about one of his plays in particular. From what I hear, their own was a copy of it.

CO: What play is that?

LUCY LAKE: *The Love Suicides at Sonezaki*. Quite famous, in Japan. They said they adored it. That was the last visit.

CO: Now, really, Miss Lake, what did you think about these two, an American Army general and his wife, doing all this?

LUCY LAKE: I thought it unutterably sad. Sobering. At their age, watching them try to find it, in poetry. They began like good children: obedient, slightly worshipful. Stealing quietly into the world of art, a magic forest they thought filled with mossy groves and dappled pastures and innocent living things. Finding, instead, pits and swamps and the true difficulties of the animals within. Sheila—oh, I tried to tell her—

CO: Please take your time.

LUCY LAKE: Well, what a waste! She must have been such a cheerful girl. Not beautiful, but—radiant, whole: a good American girl! A Navy nurse, picked up by a young Army captain, as they stood wondering in front of the great golden Buddha at Kamakura. They had just conquered Japan. So, they shacked up, took a trip.

Nikko, Nara, Fuji, the Inland Sea, everywhere. Sheila told me her young Army captain was so strong a man, she sexually adored him, but she married him because he was decent, and so very kind. They loved Japan, the Army, and each other. In twenty years, they managed to spend only seven west of Hawaii. And then, it all— well.

CO: And then?

LUCY LAKE: Oh, Jesus, General. If you don't know, how can I tell you? Ask me another!

CO [*swiftly*]: Well, I *don't* know, Miss Lake! And, yes, I certainly will ask you another. Which I hope you might answer without that attitude that bores me just as much as I obviously bore you. The General and his wife committed suicide. Do you know why?

LUCY LAKE [*swiftly*]: And if I do, and if I tell you, do you suppose I'd believe you would ever take me seriously?

CO: Well, why do you think you were asked to come here?

LUCY LAKE: Oh, because my name was on that list. For the recording session.

CO: The what?

LUCY LAKE: Recording session. That's all this is. We're his secretaries, scribes! The General has us here writing it all down for him, what he made happen. [*Pause*] Bringing his disparate elements together. [*Pause*] He must have calculated what people wouldn't understand then, they might figure out now.

CO: That may be.

47

LUCY LAKE: Got to be. [*Quickly*] Why weren't *you* there, by the way?

CO: At the Halloween party?

LUCY LAKE: Sure. You were second in command. Number two. Right?

CO: Yes.

LUCY LAKE: Well, where were you?

CO: In the field. Inspecting a supply base, on another island.

LUCY LAKE: And who sent you there?

CO: The General.

LUCY LAKE: So you could come to it with an open mind today. Sure.

CO: Perhaps. In any case, Miss Lake, believe me, whatever you have to say, I will take it seriously.

LUCY LAKE [*smiling*]: Promise?

CO: Promise.

LUCY LAKE: Okay. Ask.

CO: The General and his wife committed suicide here on this dance floor. Why?

LUCY LAKE: Because he came to believe, literally now, something dreadful. And his wife had the courage to agree with him.

CO: And what was that?

LUCY LAKE: That he was a sort of child murderer. That he had murdered his son.

[*A pause*]

CO: Miss Lake, the General's son was a grown man. A combat Marine. He was killed in action in 1965, near Danang.

LUCY LAKE: Precisely.

[*A pause. The* CO *smiles.*]

CO: Well, my dear Miss Lake.

[*A pause.* LUCY LAKE *doesn't smile.*]

LUCY LAKE: Well, my dear General.

[*A pause again. The* CO *laughs, throws up his hands.*]

Yeah, you see?

CO: What?

LUCY LAKE: You were going to take me seriously, remember?

CO: Well, I'm very sorry, but I certainly expected something more worthy of Lucy Lake.

LUCY LAKE [*coldly*]: And I expected you to keep your word.

CO [*coldly*]: I beg your pardon. You say the General believed he'd murdered his son. How? And now let me ask you to be specific.

LUCY LAKE: Well, yeah, that's the problem. We Americans so love abstractions. Adore to escape into them. Where we don't have to face the dirty details, specifics, of reality. For a while, anyhow. Well, you know Gertrude Stein held that two nations understand abstraction best, Spain and the United States.

CO: What does—

LUCY LAKE: Just hold on a minute, will you? For the Spaniard, the abstraction is ritual: bullfight, church. For the American, the abstraction is pure action: ball game, government. We worship it the way the Romans worshiped Rome, as that smart Sergeant Major understands. It is our religion. Read Gertrude Stein. Or Henry Adams, for that matter.

CO: I have, Miss Lake.

LUCY LAKE: My point is, the General began to live on a different, unfamiliar level of perception. It is not abstract. It can be very pretty, but also extremely ugly, because it relishes these specifics, and details: these dirty particular realities of existence. It has many names. Poetry is one of them. The General had to consider things that had never before crossed his mind.

CO: Such as?

LUCY LAKE: You can start with his God: his lifelong worship of abstract action. Achievement, never mind why, or for what purpose. Our national habit, etched into our beings: an achievement a day keeps the bad thoughts away. That habit, and the release it gives, is the fundamental law of the American soul, and the reason we become, so often, moral lunatics.

CO: Become so often what?

LUCY LAKE [slowly]: Mo-ral lun-a-tics.

CO: Well, speak for yourself, Miss Lake. But go ahead.

LUCY LAKE: But action, planned, considered, becomes an abstraction. Abstraction has this problem: you can es-

50

cape into it for a while, but every now and then, you get caught: somebody has to really do all those things you dreamed up, and you are obliged to step outside and see what happened while you were in there playing. The General did.

CO: But what does your subject—ah, abstract action— have to do with the General killing his son?

LUCY LAKE: It was the murder weapon. The instrument of homicide.

CO: I'm sorry. I'm quite lost.

LUCY LAKE: You don't have to tell me that.

CO [tersely]: Did the General ever actually tell you he thought he'd killed his son? Did his wife?

LUCY LAKE: Not directly, no.

CO: You never overheard him say anything like that?

LUCY LAKE: No.

CO: And, in fact, they didn't suggest to you or anyone else anything of the sort!

LUCY LAKE: No.

CO: But you—

LUCY LAKE: Still insist the General believed he had murdered his son. And his wife did, too. Yes.

[GENERAL EVANS stands up.]

EVANS: Oh, for goodness' sake!

CO: General Evans—

EVANS: General, if you please! Your command, but allow me this courtesy. One question, if I may.

CO: Miss Lake?

LUCY LAKE: Fire!

EVANS: Are you married, ma'am. Do you have any children?

LUCY LAKE: Not any more, thank God.

EVANS: Then what do you understand about it? How can you insult a good servant to his country, a wonderful father to his son? And that son, let me tell you, Mike never pushed into the service. He ran to it! They—that father and that son—were both proud of either life to be given for the United States! Just as I was! And am! Proud, ma'am!

LUCY LAKE: Bullshit, General.

EVANS [*amazed*]: What kind of a woman are you, to be so cruel? How can you say that to people who give their own children, for *your* good, and safety? What do you know about the real difficulties of military life! It's Sheila you keep talking about. Just why were you here, messing about in her life? Just what kind of a creature are you, anyway?

LUCY LAKE: If what you want to say is I'm an old-fashioned New England literary dyke, General Evans, then why don't you say it? It isn't true, but it might make you feel better, and, in any case, I have been through wars you would never have survived. Watch out or I'll blister your tin bottom for you. You speak to me with respect. Mike did.

EVANS [*icily*]: Well, I beg your pardon.

LUCY LAKE: You got it. And, of course, you're quite right. I did stay to be with Sheila. I don't often find someone I like as much as I liked her. We became, in a very short time, good, quiet friends. There are some people in the world, General, capable of that, and when they have the chance, they take it. On those afternoons by the sea, we knitted, Sheila and I, and talked about children, and poetry.

EVANS: With all personal respect, I just can't understand that! I knew them both longer and better than you did. They grieved, terribly. But they knew why their son died. They wouldn't write amateur romantic poetry about it. And they certainly wouldn't cry over it, with people like you.

[LUCY LAKE *opens her purse, takes out a sheet of paper.*]

LUCY LAKE: They gave me one. This is a sonnet. Written by both of them, each speaking to the other. Shall I?

CO: By all means.

[*Detached, calmly,* LUCY LAKE *reads their sonnet.*]

LUCY LAKE: "On Making Love Again":

But for this night and rain we wouldn't weep,
As that dear face fades slowly from our keep,
And we drink gallons, press our souls to sleep,
And in his world alone no harvest reap.
Backs again should bend, old fists be furled
As if from sperm and womb we'd simply hurled
His being, so deep in our ambition curled,
Away! Right now! into some better world.

It's dry, my love, to bear these dreams we
  seek,
And tears at night fit best the treacherous
  meek:
I've watched my heart, I know the blood-sharp
  beak
Run through it is my own: it mends next week.
But wet and heedless rain undoes the national
  spite,
And my corrupted love is yours, through rain and night.

[*Pause. She shrugs.*] The most romantic poets in the world are all in the Army.

CO: Is there anything else you have to say, Miss Lake?

LUCY LAKE: I'd like to tell General Evans something.

EVANS: Fire.

LUCY LAKE: I was married, General. Twice, years ago. Before I learned what I know about myself now. That I destroy more than I create. I, too, had a son who died. In an Ivy League university. A battlefield *he* ran to, to please me. Where he perished.

EVANS: I'm truly sorry. But that's more like it. I see it is *your* son you have talked about here today. And I understand.

LUCY LAKE: My son and yours, General. And Mike's. Ours. [*Pause. She looks about quickly, her mind racing after something.*] Wait just a minute! Has anyone else— here today—lost a son—a child—of any age—in any way?

MISS NOMURA [*nodding quietly*]: Yes. That was the General's other qualification for his private secretary.

[LUCY LAKE *looks at them all. She comes to* SERGEANT *and* MRS. BATES.]

BATES: A baby boy.

LUCY LAKE [*square at the* CO]: And how about you?

CO: Yes.

[*She stands wondering, looking at everyone sharply, in searching amazement.*]

LUCY LAKE: I told you—that man—had a feeling—for building a poem.

[*Pause. They stare at her and she stares back at them.*]

CO: Thank you, Miss Lake. Can you stay here with us a little while longer?

LUCY LAKE: Sure. I didn't see the play, either. It's my story, too. [*She steps down.*]

CO [*To* MARTIN]: Captain, I want some time. Break.

MARTIN: Ladies and gentlemen, we'll have a short break now, and begin again shortly. Thank you.

INTERMISSION

Interlude

DEPOSITION CAPTAIN HAROLD D STRETCH COMPANY COMMANDER HEAVY MORTAR COMPANY 15TH INFANTRY BRIGADE TAKEN TAPE RECORDER 11/2/70 CORPORAL HENRY T VERES MILITARY POLICE STRICKLER ARMYNAVY HOSPITAL TYPED DELIVERED READ SAME DAY SCHOFIELD BARRACKS OFFICERS CLUB INQUIRY ORDERS BRIG GEN THOMAS N BORDEN COMMANDING

No sir you must answer I have my orders

Yes I understand that but haven't the doctors told him how sick I am this burning fever there are all sorts of things wrong inside my body haven't they told him that

Doctors say you are in no danger sir and agreed to this interview technically let me repeat you don't have to say anything you don't want to but my impression is the Commanding General strongly repeat strongly desires communication from you

And you say no danger no danger God damn it I am finally I am entitled to after all these years and now this cockeyed thing to some consideration in this man's oh Jesus well what do you want me to say I'm sorry yes God Almighty of course I'm sorry but can't you just put yourself in my place for a minute

Your place

Yes my place don't look at me like that Christ you know you've done that before just horsing around pretending I

mean a good man can take a joke right no matter how God-
damn high tone a good man has got to take a joke even from
people like me right who never got the blue ribbon tied on
from the beginning and has had to do a lot of plowing
around to just get anything at all and a good joke and
while I was doing that and it was working beginning to
work everybody beginning to go with it hahaha and then
Holy Jesus Mary and Saint Joseph they are killing themselves

And what were you doing Captain please

Me well you know what I was doing everybody knows
what I was doing kneeling down there hawhawhaw and
halfway through it while I was still playing like a real baby
for sure on that thing Mama and Daddy Daddy Mamma-
mama and they're doing it to each other before baby could
even stop playing well sure *mea culpa mea culpa* maybe
I'm the God-damn Devil how do I know I just know it happened

But how did it happen if you please Captain

Well ugly yes bad taste yes but I had my dreams too
once and its not for want of good taste they came to nothing
me who wanted things once never mind what my dreams
anyway not company commander close to forty years old
playing with mortars mortars bad taste that's all I'm guilty
of how can bad taste kill anyone

Please describe what you were doing

Nothing wrong just getting to know you getting to
know all about you sure I'm the God-damn Devil all I did
was hope you know to make my impression when he took
over this Division a boneyard for me if I didn't do something I spent three months when I knew about it every night
three months every night fighting mosquitoes and flash-
light batteries learning how to play with a God-damn bow

and arrow and when I finally got it so I could hit a car at
three or four feet saluting one fine day walking past him
across the quadrangle let it slip and sure enough he bit and
the next thing I knew that weekend we were back of his
quarters and there he was with that crazy bamboo bow of
his bigger than anything I ever saw and me with my Sears,
Roebuck Special and he laughed and said none of that was
important he'd teach me teach me and I thought hot damn
I am going to get somewhere now teach me oh he taught
me all right patient nice me a God-damn baby who'd have
shot the farmer's cow if there was one around myself in
the foot put an arrow in my ear but chuga chuga boy he's
bit on me for some crazy reason and chuga chuga there I am
a little boy a baby around hero just like always sucking
Stretch sucks and well how else stay alive in the Army pay
for three wives and that last one hasn't even been around to
see me
    Captain
    Six kids they haven't been here either I'm sick
    Captain
    I'll bet they all flew to Chile or something *mea culpa*
mea culpa them with me enduring that man playing hero to
me and me having to suck that bow it was huge I mean just
a piece of bamboo but God he could use it hold that thing
and hold it and hold it and go into a weird trance crazy it
was some kind of nutball religion to him the whole thing
and Captain Harold D. Sambo here sucking and sucking
and lucky to get an arrow out of my God-damn bow string
without slapping myself in the face with it but patience
patience Stretch come on now he said and *mea culpa* but he
was a major general and me a desperate man Jesus Mary
and Saint Joseph while he said patience Stretch now attend
attend trying to show me crazy things pagan nuts like you

have to be losing yourself to hit the target forgetting yourself to hit the target in fact you are the target and the arrow
and you are hit while you release the arrow and its all peaceful and you don't think no hell no I don't think I didn't have
time I was sucking him so hard until he said peaceful and
you don't think you are the flight and the arrow and the
archer and the hit son that's when I stopped sucking son son
son he was playing me like I was his God-damn little kid or
something me a grown man even if a miserable old suck-up
still and all a man and that was the bottom I never thought
I'd ever find it but I did when he used a desperate man like
me to be a daddy to and teach him to be the arrow and the
target and I wanted to break that God-damn crazy bamboo
bow over his head and still tried and tried until he just
stopped one fine day and looked at me queerly and said *You
are just not getting the hang of this are you Captain sorry I
should be impatient with you my fault* and that was all
dropped dropped no more bows and arrows and me tearing
my hair out by the roots to see if it did any good and last
month finding out not a bit he didn't do a thing for me after
all that sucking playing sonny Japanese bow string suck
with him all that time and nothing for it no way out a captain still and nothing more and the Army can kick me out
anytime and it is fine with him so it is wrong you see what
he did to me

What he did to you Captain

Yes yes they should have waited let me make a fool of
myself and go home and then if they had to oh Jesus listen
Christ in heaven above and Our Lady of Sorrows but how
do you think I feel about it

How did you feel Captain then I mean tell us please

In bad taste I felt in bad taste but I mean you take a
joke in this country don't you and hell it was funny at first

and I was getting something off right at last a good shot
finally and him the God-damn target this time not little
Harold Stretch all the jokes played on him you betcha God-
damn painful all-American murder what the hell is bad
taste anyway and why did they do that to me I got to sleep
now this fever I am burning up they set me on fire and I
burning everybody has to take a joke how else do you get
along when everything is impossible anyway and I didn't
mean them any harm

Doctor speaking Corporal I think that's enough

Corporal speaking yes sir

Captain Stretch speaking not with all these things
wrong inside my body the Devil didn't mean them any harm

Act Two

———⊸•⊷———

[*The people assemble. The inquiry continues.*]

MARTIN: Robert J. Yankman, please.

[*No response*]

Robert J. Yankman, please?

[*No response*]

CO: Who is he, Captain?

MARTIN: Mr. Yankman is president of a savings and loan association in Honolulu, sir.

LUCY LAKE: He's also running for governor of Hawaii. You expect him to be *here?*

CO: Proceed, Captain. Thank you, Miss Lake.

LUCY LAKE: Sure.

MARTIN: Colonel Robertson H. Moore.

MOORE: Well, I'm here, anyway, God help me. [*He takes the stand: a thin, healthy, sardonic man.*] And I do understand the nature of this inquiry, et cetera, et cetera, and I am Robertson H. Moore, Colonel, Chief of Staff, this Division, and I know exactly why the General got me down on his little list, and why I'm here, and what I'm supposed to say, and I'll be just delighted to say it.

63

CO [*smiling*]: All right, Robie. Go right ahead.

MOORE: A pleasure. With all respect to Lucy Lake, I am here to give the minority report, my usual function. I really don't mean to dance on the man's grave, but I suppose I disagreed with the General on just about every idea he ever had. The only thing I approved was the way he played poker. That he knew how to do. And his archery, of course. But tennis, his mind collapsed every second set. And golf, now, a game of fidelity and endurance, well, to watch him go to pieces inside a constant framework, under stern and unchanging rules, well, it was to realize that he was a profoundly childish man. It sometimes passes for intelligence. Sorry, ladies and gentlemen, but that's the freezing truth.

CO: And just what we want you to say, Robie. Go on.

MOORE: You really don't have to call me "Robie." Little telegrams are no doubt replacing both of us at the moment: you as executive officer and heir apparent, and me as his ridiculous chief of staff. He appointed me above my time in rank, and kept me there against my wishes. He also started calling me "Robie," with nauseating condescension.

CO: I beg your pardon, Colonel. Your record speaks for itself. You've been very effective.

MOORE: Well, I do have my passion for details. Okay. But that isn't why he kept me there, over the heads of at least five other officers. He made me his chief of staff because I was a thorn in his side. Due to the chemistry of our personalities, or whatever, I could never lie to him. Or flatter him. He kept me with him because I always told him what I thought of his decisions, and him. And I disapproved of *that* more than anything.

CO: You disapproved of a superior officer who allowed you to speak honestly to him?

MOORE: Of course! That isn't the way this army or any other army works, and you know it and I know it and he knew it! As a matter of fact, it isn't the way *anything* works, as *everybody* knows! But it was his perverse nature to be—well, illustration, please. May I? I mean, I won't be sued for slander, will I?

CO: You won't be sued for slander, Colonel.

MOORE: Fine. That Italian place down the pike, you know, was his favorite off-post restaurant. It's pretty dependent on the military, so of course the waiters all peed in their britches every time he walked in the door. Okay, fine. But you see, he made them play it the other way around. They had to joke with him—ha ha—and pick on him and kid him and *bully* him a little, you know— ho ho—so he could be just one of the boys there. Another good fellow, who belongs, and who'd get it, just like anybody else, if he stepped out of line. Christ, you half expected him to go out and lay some bricks with them on weekends. Pals, real sports, and it was pathetic to watch him. Sickening. You might have respected the man if he'd made those flunkies bang their heads on the floor and run their tails off when they brought him his Chateaubriand—I think he hated Italian food—but watching him play that game with them made me want to vomit. Because that's what *I* was! Honest, outspoken, independent. Chief of Staff, nothing, I was his flunkey Italian waiter, and I hated it, and him. Tyrants, who still have to pretend to be regular fellows. Is that universal, or another one of Lucy Lake's fundamental laws of the American soul?

LUCY LAKE: Both.

MOORE: I guess. Well, the General was that kind of tyrant, who couldn't let you go until you shook hands with him, and told him you didn't blame him a bit for cutting out your gizzard. That was his only principle. Not to be blamed. [*To* LUCY LAKE] That's where he was a poet, and a good one.

CO: All right, Colonel Moore. You've filed your minority report. Did you have any specific confrontation with him just before the incident?

MOORE: Well, I fought with him damn near every day, you know, so I hold out to you an embarrassment of riches. But the biggest fight we had, and the gem, was, of course, about the President.

CO: President?

MOORE: Yes. Of the United States. Yes.

CO: Ah. You mean the conference?

MOORE: That's right. That was called off. That's right.

CO: Well, what about it?

MOORE: As everybody knows, late last month the President of the United States announced another Hawaiian conference with the president of our noble allies in Indochina. Word had come down to the General almost six weeks ago, September 25th. Same old thing. Three days of the President in Hawaii. The General had a fit.

co: Why?

moore: Oh, God knows. He was full of little explosions, you know. He bitched and raved about the preparations involved, when of course the President would never come within thirty miles of Schofield. Then he said the hell with it, and left the paperwork to me. Okay. Five days later, with steam coming out of his ears, he wanted to know why the hell our contingency plans for the arrival in Hawaii of the Commander in Chief weren't smoldering red-hot on his desk. Because you said the hell with it, I said. So he hopped all over me, and I hopped and we both hopped.

co: Why the sudden change in attitude? Duty?

moore: Hardly. The General's idea of his military duty was much too sophisticated to include anything as simple as obedience. No, what had happened was brand new. Army Headquarters had now scheduled the President, if he felt like it on Saturday night, to visit Schofield Barracks and attend the Annual Officers' Club Halloween Party. Now, the General thought that was just dandy, so we worked like hell.

co: But that conference was called off.

moore: Right. Poof. *Fini.* No Hawaiian conference with Indochina. No Halloween with the President. The General, surprise, after all that work, wasn't angry. No, he had a strange, dippy, far-off look in his eyes, as if he was dreaming about something impossible, and he said, "Well, we'll just pretend he came, and have the party anyway." And that was that.

[*A pause*]

CO: Interesting.

[*Pause*]

MOORE: Yes, isn't it.

[*Pause*]

CO: Well, Colonel, were there any other confrontations you wanted to tell us about?

MOORE: You don't get it, do you?

CO: Get what, Colonel?

MOORE: Never mind! Neither do I. Nothing more I have to say. Except I was here Saturday night, and saw it, and I find most extraordinary the justice of it. I still can't believe he did it, but he gave himself exactly what he deserved.

CO: Now, Robie!

MOORE [*quickly*]: Sorry! I didn't mean that. Forgive the attitude. But you see, it's hard being a United States Army colonel and an Italian waiter at the same time. Sorry. [*He steps down.*]

MARTIN: Mrs. Norvel T. Bates, please.

[*An attractive woman, in her late thirties, takes the stand. She is very decorous and proper.*]

Mrs. Bates, this inquiry does not require you to answer if you don't want to. Is that clear?

MRS. BATES: Yes, sir.

MARTIN: You are Lorna Ann Bates, and you are married to Master Sergeant Norvel T. Bates, Headquarters Company, this Division?

MRS. BATES: Yes, sir, I am.

MARTIN: You reside here at Schofield, in Army housing, with your husband and his two children.

MRS. BATES: Yes, sir, I do.

MARTIN: Mrs. Bates, you are in charge of the reorganized and enlarged Schofield Children's Day Care Center, for which, this summer, you received the Post Civilian Award for outstanding service to Schofield Barracks?

MRS. BATES: That's right, yes, sir.

MARTIN: You are also recording secretary of the Schofield Ladies' Garden Club and a member of the Schofield Ladies' Aid Association?

MRS. BATES [*quietly*]: Yes, sir.

MARTIN: Mrs. Bates, is it true that the expansion of the Children's Day Care Center was the General's idea?

MRS. BATES: Oh, yes. His and his wife's. There wasn't much to it until they came.

CO [*smiling*]: And brought you.

MRS. BATES: And brought me, yes, sir.

MARTIN: Mrs. Bates, we have no particular questions here to ask you. By your name the General noted that you would know what to tell us, and that he hoped you would. Do you understand what he meant?

MRS. BATES: Yes, I'm afraid I do.

MARTIN: Are you willing, then, to talk about it?

MRS. BATES: I guess I have to. If that's what he wanted. Like I say, everything at the Children's Center was just wonderful until about two weeks ago. Then they took to coming to the playground together, every day. Something was different about them. I don't know how to describe it. They just stood there by the fence, watching. Then, about ten days ago, they told me they wanted a child.

MARTIN: I beg your pardon?

MRS. BATES: They said they wanted a child, for the Halloween party. A little boy, old enough to stay up late.

MARTIN: What was your answer?

MRS. BATES: To them? We have twelve children four afternoons a week. Mostly Eurasian mothers, GI fathers, abandoned by both parents. They're sent here to us for the chance to mix and play with other children. I called, and it was all right.

MARTIN: Called who?

MRS. BATES: The orphanage. They said as long as the General and his wife were responsible, of course. So I introduced them to a new little friend we have: Yoshida Robinson. Yoshi is six and a half. They came to see him every day after that, with some little present or other. They played with him, and read him stories, and even rehearsed his part in their play. I never got to see that. They wanted to keep it a secret.

CO: Now, wait a minute! You don't mean they meant for the child to be in *that* play? In which they committed suicide?

MRS. BATES [*very unhappy*]: Well, yes, in a way I suppose they did, but——

70

EVANS: Mrs. Bates, are you telling us that this child, an orphan, was being prepared by the General and his wife to take some part in their act of violence? Their *deaths?*

MRS. BATES: No, of course they wouldn't do anything like that! No! But—Yoshi was supposed to have been there, and was, and except for me—

CO: Except for you, Mrs. Bates?

MRS. BATES: Yes. Me. I let them down, you see. I got Yoshi out of there before it happened.

CO: Be glad you did. But why in the world would they involve a child in this terrible thing?

MRS. BATES: I don't know! And it makes them look bad, and that's wrong! They wouldn't have upset Yoshi for anything. But—well, I had Yoshi here all right, but when they came walking in, all dressed like they were and acting so strange—well I just couldn't let a child get mixed up with anything like that. So I told Mrs. Ernest Snow, who helps at the Center, I said, "Ruth, take Yoshi out of here," and she did. And when they came to the part in that play where they called for him, there wasn't no child there. And that horrible man, that Captain Stretch, he saw me send Yoshi home, and he knew then there wouldn't be any child there, and got the idea for that awful joke he played on them. After all they done for me, I let them down!

MOORE [*breaking in*]: All they did for you, Mrs. Bates, was use you. Don't you see what kind of people they really were?

MRS. BATES [*very upset*]: That's not true! You—what do you know about it?

CO: Well, Mrs. Bates, they did in fact involve you, and through you, a child, in an act of violence. Why?

MRS. BATES: I don't know why! But this is all wrong, me making them look so bad! And after I let them down, let them down!

CO: Mrs. Bates, you didn't let anybody down. You prevented what looks like some wanton act of cruelty.

MRS. BATES [*horrified*]: *Cruel? Them?* [*She breaks down.*] Aw, *shit!* [*There is a shocked silence. She jumps out of her chair, goes to her husband,* SERGEANT BATES, *and puts her hands on his shoulders. Her extreme anguish is puzzling.*] Oh, Norvel.

SERGEANT BATES: Lorna, go on and say what you want to say.

MRS. BATES: It ain't going to do no good.

SERGEANT: That's all right. Say it.

CO: Mrs. Bates, you have absolutely everybody's respect. Nothing you can say will change that.

[*She looks at him and at the people, her attitude and personality shifting. She takes her seat again, staring at everyone, something in her now quite coarse and tough.*]

MRS. BATES: You think so? We'll see.

CO: Please.

MRS. BATES: I met them first outside Miami, at a place

called Slim's, on Route 1. Dinah Shore and Jerry Lewis don't play Slim's, but I did. That was in the summer of 1966. I was thirty-five long American years old, and I thought I had seen all the ugly, low-down American things a girl like me could see. I wrote a song about that. Used to sing it, with my Star-Spangled Garter-Belt Guitar: "I'm Highway born and Highway bred, I'll be Highway shed, and Highway dead." I'll sing it for you sometime, at the Ladies' Club. Well, that night, I was just back from the Dominican Republic, where I'd been for a while, with a real nice man I knew. Brought back an act with a snake, and a few other things. Like smashing customers' beer bottles in a big towel and opening the towel and rolling around stripping in the broken glass, and not getting cut. "Not one little bit, on one pretty tit! No, sir, not even one cut, on this big bouncing butt!" Things like that I learned for a living, and playing with snakes, and men. I didn't even see them come in. They were just there, sitting at the piano bar, when I came back out, dressed. They were wearing just plain old clothes, of course, and just wanted a quiet, relaxing, low-down bar sort of a drink. They could get awful tired, you know, of Officers' Clubs and official parties they had to go to. [*She smiles, fondly.*] Oh, we had a time that night. They stayed; and we sang a lot, and drank a lot, and had the best time together. They even sent me a Christmas card that winter, and we wrote now and then, and about two years ago they wrote asking where I'd be that summer, and they came to see me. "Hello," they said. "Hello," I said. They didn't ask why I was at Freedom Ranch, in Calcutta, California, which is a Western-style mental encounter group–type whorehouse, because they knew. I was working, like before.

This time I was the house masseuse. I had aged, you see, just slightly. "Say, friends, if anybody feels like an informal massage after therapy, just call the house girl, Lorna, the prostate professional. Give you a spurt that sure can't hurt." "Hello," they said. "Hello," I said. "You're looking fine," they said. "Oh, yes," I said, "I've come up in the world. High society, now." "Any different?" they asked. "No," I said. "Same old Highway trash. Better clothes, and the pimps have Ph.D.'s." And they laughed, and that was the night, because of so many things, I don't know, it came to an end for me, and I swallowed everything I had in the medicine cabinet, and went to sleep dreaming of my first husband, my childhood sweetheart I married in Plainfield, Kansas, who when he got mad at me used to fry my brassière and panties in the oven, and I did sleep, and I was gone away from it all, a free American at last, at peace, and then, oh, God, stomach pumps, and a knife in my brains, and a thermometer up my ass. And the General and his wife, who'd been concerned about me, I was told, and who'd saved my life. "Why?" I asked them, when I saw them at my bedside. He was dressed right then. It was the first time I'd seen him in his uniform, strong and clean and proud and a real man. "Because, Lorna," he said, "you are a decent girl, and we know that, and we're your friends." And they were. They kept up with me when I got out of the hospital, and wrote to me a lot, and after a while they did what they'd come to see me about. They got Norvel and me together. Norvel was lost, too, at that time, with no wife any more, and two children to care for alone, and so we were married. After almost forty years, I was saved. Like in the storybooks. Saved from the ditch, from the rock-bottom Highway trash of these United States. [*She looks about, filled with anger and anguish.*] And now they've gone and done what they saved me from! They have killed themselves, like I tried to do. And everybody wonders why. Well, Jesus Christ on the Cross, I'll tell you why! They were too God-damned good for their own stinking country, that's why, and after fifty years of believing in it, they found that out! [*Crying*] I could have told them that! I knew that! They didn't have to die for that! God damn it! [*She stands up.*] Not until the very end did I know what they was going to do, and then I just stood there, saying, "Don't, oh don't." But they did. The plain, good life they gave me, they couldn't keep for themselves. [*She stares out at everyone with defiance.*] Because it is the Army that is the most decent thing about this country. Everything else in it I ever seen is shit. And the General, except for the husband he found for me, is the only top-to-bottom real man I ever met. Or ever will. [*She smiles, bitterly.*] I would be happy to work forever at the Day Care Center. I am proud of my Schofield Civilian Award. But I know everything will change now, and never be the same. But my husband, and his children, and me, we will be all right. What the General and the Army gave to me, this country cannot never take back away from me again. Never. That's what they meant to me, the General and his wife.

CO: Thank you.

MRS. BATES: Yes, sir. [*She steps down. There is a pause while she sits by her husband, very decorous and proper again.*]

[*A telephone at* MARTIN's *table rings.* MARTIN *answers.*]

MARTIN: Captain Martin. Yes, sir, he's right here.

[*The* CO *picks up his phone.*]

CO: Yes? All right, put him on. [*Pause*] No, sir. I have gone ahead with it. [*Pause*] Yes, sir, that was my decision. The order was technically correct. [*Pause*] Yes, General Evans is right here. [*He holds out the phone to* EVANS.] For you, sir.

EVANS: Evans. [*Pause*] Right. No, don't do that yet. [*He hangs up and returns to his seat.*]

CO: Next?

[MARTIN *is now quite nervous. He checks his list with the* CO, *pointing to the next name.*]

Call her.

MARTIN: Miss Judith Borden, please.

[*A very plain, impish college girl, with mischief in her eyes, steps forward. She stops before going to the witness chair.*]

MISS BORDEN [*to* MARTIN]: I am Judith Borden.

MARTIN: Would you take the stand, please, Miss Borden?

MISS BORDEN: Perhaps. I do have information to contribute. But I want my friend to stay with me.

MARTIN: I beg your pardon? Stay—

MISS BORDEN: With me. Physically with me. Stand by me when I talk.

MARTIN [*looking at the* CO]: Why—ah—

CO [*sternly*]: Permitted. Agreed.

[*Her friend, a young student her own age, steps forward.*]

MARTIN [*very uncomfortable*]: All right, Miss Borden. And you, sir, you are—

MISS BORDEN: A friend.

[*They both go to the witness chair. She sits, and he stands beside and slightly behind her, one hand resting lightly on her shoulder.*]

MARTIN: You are Judith Borden, and you are nineteen years old?

MISS BORDEN: Twenty.

MARTIN: Twenty. You are a junior at the University of Hawaii?

MISS BORDEN: Yes.

MARTIN: You live on the campus, at Susan Campbell Hall for—

MISS BORDEN: Not any more. Now I live with my friend.

MARTIN [*flustered, stammering*]: Ah—I see. And you are related— [*Quickly*] I mean, connected with this—

MISS BORDEN: I knew the General, and especially his wife. She was an Army brat once, as I am now. I saw her often this summer, when I lived here with my father, who is now the Commanding General. [*For the first time, she looks at the* CO, *mischief dancing in her eyes.*] Hello, Daddy.

77

co: Hello, Judy.

MARTIN [*hapless*]: Ah, yes—well—

co: Thank you, Lieutenant Martin. You've cleared my path now, and I think I can proceed. [*To his daughter*] Shall I call you Judy, or shall it be Miss Borden?

MISS BORDEN [*wryly*]: Would you rather it be General Borden, or shall I call you Daddy?

co [*quickly*]: General.

MISS BORDEN [*quickly*]: Miss.

co: Fine. Miss Borden, in his embarrassment, the Captain forgot to tell you—

MISS BORDEN: I don't have to say anything I don't want to. Understood.

co: Let me add that that includes anything personal about me. Leave it out, or put it in.

MISS BORDEN: All right. Thank you.

co: Not at all. My note tells me there was one meeting this summer between the three of you. That's all. And I don't remember your mentioning it to me.

MISS BORDEN: No. That is because, for some time now, I haven't known where you were, or who you were. What you believed in, or didn't believe in, or if you believed in anything at all. And we have not been— comfortable—together.

co: Correct.

MISS BORDEN: Well, I never talked about that meeting, but I will now. I have been trying to make a transition: from Army brat to history major. The General's wife encouraged me. So does my friend, who tells me if I take your money for school, I should do something honorable with it.

CO: Please thank him for me.

MISS BORDEN: I will.

CO: And come to the point.

MISS BORDEN: One night this July. The General was in Washington and New York. Not at home.

CO: Right.

MISS BORDEN: His wife asked me over, to talk about a man I've fallen in love with. He was the first man to stand up on the floor of the Senate and oppose slavery. Daniel Webster wouldn't do that. He did. He insisted prisons be reformed, too. His speeches were scathing, and, for that, once he was beaten bloody at his Senate desk, while many laughed and watched. They said he was a pompous, harsh fool, the kind of man who would bring on a civil war if he didn't shut up. But Lincoln wanted him chairman of the Foreign Relations Committee. But he fought with Lincoln, too, defeated his bills, and I believe he forced Lincoln to the Emancipation Proclamation. He denounced Ulysses Grant, too, when he was President, and for that was stripped of all his power. He died in 1874, fighting for his civil-rights bill, and at his grave stood Emerson and Longfellow, and Oliver Wendell Holmes, and Frederick Douglass.

CO: Miss Borden, if you please—

MISS BORDEN: There *is* a point! Indulge me, Daddy, as the General asked.

CO: Of course I will indulge you. But you aren't just testifying to me, Judy.

MISS BORDEN: No. That is always hard for me to remember. But I will.

CO: Do.

MISS BORDEN: For years teachers and historians have dismissed him: a fool. But I fell in love with my neurotic, ungainly, overeducated, pompous hothouse orator. I told the General's wife that. I defended all his actions, and quoted his speeches. I told her all the unhappy things about his personality, how egotistical he was, how wretched he was, and how much I loved him because what he said was right; he wasn't another charlatan, it *was* right, and I am dying, dying, to find *something* I can respect! And I don't mean a great Astronaut, or a great Preacher, or a great Novelist, or a great Revolutionary, or a great Voluptuary, or a great General of the Army. Or any kind of American success like that! Well, all that time, the General was there. He was sitting in a rocker on the porch, listening to me through the living-room window, his flight bag at his feet. This is what he heard. Charles Sumner, the man's name, when he was young made a Fourth of July speech on the Boston Common. Oh, terribly verbose and oratorical. A three-hour oration against war. Safe enough? Well, not quite. He called it "The True Grandeur of Nations"; people said its real title should have been "The True Grandeur of Sumner." Nevertheless, my friend and I have much of it by heart. Friend?

[*The young man at her side speaks. Calmly, naturally, directly, to the Army officers around him, and his calm, defiant attitude gives just a touch of the vanished power of American oratory.*]

FRIEND: What, in our age, is true national glory—national honor—what is the true grandeur of nations? I say, in our age, there can be no peace that is not honorable; there can be no war that is not dishonorable. But the contagion spreads among us.

MISS BORDEN: His audience was filled with soldiers. Army, Navy. Officers from West Point, in dazzling uniform. We were about to invade Mexico, and rob her blind. It was their day. But listen to Sumner.

FRIEND: What is the purpose of the Standing Army of the United States? No man aware of human dignity can observe without mortification the discipline, the drilling, the marching and counter-marching, the putting of guns to the shoulder and the dropping them to earth, these farcical and humiliating exercises, which fill the lives of the poor soldiers, and trains them into parts of a mere machine. This is not a healthy, vigilant police, this is an immense system, spreading over the whole country. It is time the people declared the Army to be an utterly useless branch of the public service, a seminary of idleness and vice, uncongenial with the true institutions of this Republic. We have cultivated a military spirit, and lavished the riches, begrudged to the purposes of Peace, in preparation for War. We are not the preservers of peace. We are the provokers of war.

EVANS: Oh, that's ridiculous!

MISS BORDEN: Yes, ridiculous! And thirty years later, when he died in Washington, his ridiculous civil-rights bill died with him, to be reborn again in 1954. That Supreme Court decision was based on an argument by Charles Sumner! You have to be a fool, and do something! Listen to a fool!

FRIEND [*calmly*]: And I hear the skeptical note of some defender of the order of things, who wishes to fight for peace. Saying, these views are beautiful, but visionary, the world is not yet prepared for their reception. I say, nothing can be beautiful that is not true, and the time is now come for their reception. Now is the day and now is the hour.

MISS BORDEN: And while I was reading that to his wife, the General came into his house. He was very upset. He looked at me as if I was some loathsome bug. He asked me to leave, and I did. Last week, I got this letter from the General's wife, which can tell you something, Daddy, about how they really felt. I want to read it to you now.

CO: All right.

MISS BORDEN [*reading*]: My dear Judy—

[*Commotion. A man outside is arguing with the guards. He wants to come right in, and is making a huge fuss.*]

CO: Just a moment, please. Captain, who *is* that?

MARTIN: Sir, I'll see. [*He goes to look.*]

CO [*to his daughter*]: Sorry for the interruption.

MISS BORDEN: It's quite all right.

82

MARTIN [*returning*]: Sir, it's Mr. Roundhouse, the owner of the restaurant. Who wasn't here before. He wants in now.

ROUNDHOUSE [*loudly*]: Now! Yeah, right now!

CO [*to his daughter*]: Do you mind? I promise I'll come back to you.

MISS BORDEN: I hope so, Daddy.

[*She and her friend move to one side.* MARTIN *signals to guards, and now* EDWARD ROUNDHOUSE *enters. He is a startling, contradictory character. Fat, well scrubbed, jolly and masculine-looking. He wears Hawaiian tourist clothes, but well worn and comfortable —tennis shoes, denim trousers, a loud Aloha shirt and an enormous yellow straw hat, native-made, with a wide brim dangling shreds of straw. He has a very elegant silver liquor flask with him. He is tipsy, but in control. He comes in warily now, looking at everyone carefully. He has never set foot on the Post before. He spots the* CO.]

ROUNDHOUSE: Are you the—ah—big—ah—thing here?

CO: I am the Commanding Officer, yes.

ROUNDHOUSE: How do you do. I am Roundhouse, Edward E. I wasn't going to come to this business, but I had a drink and changed my mind. Is that all right?

CO: If you please, yes.

ROUNDHOUSE: I do please. Do I sit here? [*He does.*]

[*The* CO *motions to* MARTIN.]

MARTIN: This is an informal inquiry, that's all. The General left us a note saying you were an old friend. That you would have something to say to us.

ROUNDHOUSE: Quite right.

MARTIN: You are the owner of a restaurant on the island?

ROUNDHOUSE: Several, now. Because Michael placed me in the first one, in the early fifties, when he was a major, stationed briefly here. Its title was Michael's idea: "The Breeze and I." He found it for me, helped me buy into the place, where I swept the floor and washed the dishes until it became a lunch stop for tour buses from Waikiki. Now I'm rich. A dreadful place at noon, lovely at night. I hope none of you will come and spoil it. Now you must ask me what I did before sweeping the floors of The Breeze and I.

CO [*coldly*]: Ask him.

MARTIN [*coldly*]: What did you do before sweeping floors at The Breeze and I?

ROUNDHOUSE [*warmly*]: I was president of two American universities. After a very distinguished education in classical studies—my doctoral thesis was the superiority of Xenophon over Plato as a true gauge of the character of Socrates—I graced several advanced faculties, and in due process, bored finally with Xenophon and Socrates, turned my hand to university administration. Then, in 1945, I became president of Triton College in Ohio, and in 1951 president of the University of the Southwest. In 1952, I began sweeping the floors of The Breeze and I.

MARTIN [*floored*]: Why—ah—

ROUNDHOUSE [*nodding calmly*]: Um-hum. Quite right.
Now, allow me. In those lost days of my academic
glory, I traveled, often. I met Michael and Sheila in
1950, on that great sweeping porch of the Zen temple
that overlooks the Ryuanji Stone Gardens, outside
Kyoto. I had been to Provence and Finland, where I'd
met Sibelius and Somerset Maugham. Michael and
Sheila were also charming, on vacation, too. On my
way home, I stayed a week with them, here. We became friends. They were so eager to please me, and
to hear about the great world I traveled in so freely.
Then, time up, I returned home, to give my incoming
freshman class my most stirring speech on the advan-
tages of being an American, of the endless possibilities
thereinto appertaining, of their duty to the very best in
themselves, and after that promptly took myself to New
York, and in a perfectly respectable hotel bar I met a
young man who thought me equally charming. We ad-
journed to my room, where he turned out, of course,
to be cruising for the Vice Squad. He arrested me, that
little Benedict Arnold, whose legs, by the way, I can
still remember, O Perversity of Memory. Those were
the days of terror, you recall, when you were probably
not merely a homosexual, debauching poor innocent
policemen, but also most likely a Communist, since
both vices were obviously intimately connected. When
I got out of jail, what the Hearst papers in Chicago
didn't do to me, the faculty and board of trustees at the
University of the Southwest did. All a kind of hideous
joke now, except that it killed my mother. Contrary to
what you are told in the Dell edition of Freud, I was
very fond of her. But there I was, Mama dead as mut-
ton, buried, and, with her, my distinguished career in

higher education, which had educated only, alas, myself. I vaguely supposed I would go to Paris, call myself Sebastian Melmoth, and die there like Oscar Wilde. But my little Major Michael contacted me, and said, "Listen, I have a better idea. Come here." I did have some capital left, and with Michael's help I bought my little restaurant by the sea. And as Michael foresaw, the tidal wave of tourists rolled over me. So here I am, like a character from one of those beautiful South Sea Tales of the Master, ironically happier than ever, a closet queen Midwestern college president, turned into a rich, free comber of Somerset Maugham beaches, and boys. I am even a force in the economics of this state now, where, believe me, when there is money to be made, you can be as queer as a turtle and nobody will say a word. [*He smiles, takes a sip from his silver flask.*]

Michael didn't do it just for me. We made a deal. "Take this place, and save yourself with it," he said. And in return I was to make The Breeze and I, in the evenings only, a certain kind of place for certain soldiers of the Army this young Major so deeply loved. Not a rendezvous for the ordinary, lusty, perfectly healthy Army/Navy queer, but a place for those inducted who so often languished in lonely, sensitive, crucifying sexual despair. A haven where they might forget the terrible fears that made them so miserable in uniform, cowards, in perpetual physical disgrace. "They are good men, too," Michael said. "The Army should help them. You should help them." "Deal!" I said. So I put Offenbach in my jukebox; draped, with fiendish cunning, fish nets and sailcloth on the walls and ceiling; arranged booths for dignified semiprivacy, and created

86

what Michael had wanted. At noon, of course, I made a living, the place jammed with Los Angeles dentists and their fat wives, bedlam, yet profitable, and at night under an Oahu moon, something else. It's been that way now twenty years. The soldiers have changed some, but a few still come at night to hear Offenbach and Debussy on a jukebox, and find a man who can talk to them about the odes of Horace and the hidden music of Pindar. The last such soldier to arrive—in desperation, too, and by far the most dramatic—was Major Michael himself, now Major General Michael, who had not been to see me much lately. But he came to me one night last July, looking like death.

MISS BORDEN [*excited*]: Excuse me! What night was that, please?

ROUNDHOUSE: Pretty girl. It was a Thursday night, in July. I forget the date.

MISS BORDEN: That was the same night! The same night, Daddy!

CO: All right. [*To* ROUNDHOUSE] Please continue.

ROUNDHOUSE: After a swig. Mind?

CO: No.

ROUNDHOUSE: Thank you. [*He drinks.*] Ah, well, his face was death itself. I never saw a man more frightened. I quickly closed everything up. We sat at the bar, alone. He was dying. "Oh, God, I'm dying," he said. "I am going to die." "Ah, yes, yes," I said, "I remember. What's happened to you, Michael?" And he told me, and in time I became frightened, too.

MISS BORDEN: In New York! Something happened to him on that trip! Isn't that it?

ROUNDHOUSE: Pretty girl, with brains. Yes. How did you know?

MISS BORDEN: I saw him that night, too. I thought it was just me who upset him so.

ROUNDHOUSE [*smiling*]: A common delusion of pretty girls with brains. No, my dear, there were a few other things on his mind that night.

MISS BORDEN: Oh, what? Stop camping around and tell us!

ROUNDHOUSE [*seriously*]: His manhood. He had lost it. Not sexually. His defeat was much worse, much deeper than that. He had been called to Washington as an expert in guerrilla tactics. Michael's field inventions, I understand, were highly respected. But in Washington, he said, the squabbling, and the lying, the debased maneuvers made those conferences like the rubbing of dead shad together. Disgusted, worn out, he went to New York for a weekend by himself. He bought a tuxedo, and one night went alone to the Metropolitan Opera at Lincoln Center. He said he had a grand time. But going home—alone—he made the wrong turn, and was headed toward upper Broadway. Suddenly three men were walking with him. They swept him into a side street and into an alley between two buildings, where it was very dark. They were flawless, he said. The knife at his throat was perfectly placed. In seconds, they had squatted him down, crossed his legs, bent him over. Such skill. Coat, glasses, wristwatch, shoes, billfold. His head almost touched the sidewalk, so he could

not see them, but he knew they were not crude hood-
lums. They were trained, and very thorough. He knew
exactly what they were doing. He had trained them
himself! They had all been *soldiers!* When they saw
his identification, that he was a general, they laughed,
and one pressed the knife harder into his throat. "I
thought they were going to kill me," he said. "And
cross-legged, in my own country, like all the wretched
prisoners taken all over the world, I felt I was going
to die. And I said: 'Please don't. Don't kill me. Let me
live.'" [*A long drink*] "Cowardice. The final disgrace
of the soldier, who will kill Genghis Khan from an air-
plane and then beg on the ground for his own life, like
any poor peasant, like me." [*Another drink*] "Well, my
dear Michael," I said. "What can I do for you? Here,
in the Temple of Cowardice you so thoughtfully built
for your sensitive soldiers years ago. What?" "Find
something for me in your books," he said. "It's in those
Greek plays."

EVANS: *Ajax!* Right?

ROUNDHOUSE: Right. My God, pretty girls and generals,
all with brains. Yes, *Ajax*. We read till we found a passage he wanted to learn by heart, and I translated it
for him. He said he had seen it once before, by an open
window, copied out in the handwriting of the first
American Secretary of Defense. It is a choral ode, just
before the hero falls upon his sword:

> *Has ek patroas haykon, genias aristos—*
> Now, when the pride of this our noble race,
> Wanders, distraught, in darkness and disgrace,
> When honor's day has set in cold decay,

Better to go and sleep, than linger on,
When the life of the soul is gone.

Farewell, my best beloved, by inward Furies
    torn,
I leave the deepest, bitterest curse
This ancient, honorable house has ever borne!

I watched that man's conversion. Religions come and go, conversion remains. I saw it touch him, as fire roasts a pig on a luau spit, the flames piercing through to the organs, and burning away, in that conversion, the great soldier he had always been. I loved him. I admired him. In an age where everyone else is innocent, Michael claimed the terrible right to be guilty. Did he do it here? Right here?

CO: He did.

ROUNDHOUSE: Was it grand? Was it worthy of Ajax? That's what he wanted. God, I wish I'd seen it!

CO: So did he, Mr. Roundhouse. Please have a seat here with us. Captain.

MARTIN: Yes, sir?

CO: How did it work out?

MARTIN: Sir, with some help, we have been able to simulate the event. It should provide a fair idea of what happened.

CO: Okay. Mike would have no complaints about you, Captain.

MARTIN: Thank you, sir.

co: Crank it up.

MARTIN: Sergeant Bates, Miss Nomura, would you please take the positions you were in on Saturday night.

[*They move to the edges of the small stage.* MARTIN *hands each of them one of* BOWERS' *transcriptions of the entertainment.*]

MARTIN: And please do just what you did Saturday night. And when it's time for the General and his wife to speak, will you please read that, too?

MISS NOMURA: Very well.

BATES: Yes, sir.

[*Puzzled and apprehensive,* GENERAL EVANS *interrupts.*]

EVANS: Wait just a minute. Crank up what, may I ask?

co: Sir, in this directive, the General orders a re-enactment of their play, as they performed it on Saturday night while the tape of what actually happened is playing.

EVANS: And you really mean to do that? To them? To Mike and Sheila? Here and now?

co: It is my duty, General!

EVANS: A duty you are choosing, General, and for *your* reasons as well as his! You're not bound by the orders of a dead man, and you know it! It's perfectly obvious what has happened here. The horrors of honor are a part of the horrors of war. When you put on your country's uniform you accept that!

co: Sir, I am going ahead with it.

EVANS: General, I have loved these people all my life. But they were casualties of war, and that's all they were. What you've been doing here discredits you, them, the Army, and the United States. You will show this man some gratitude and stop, right now.

CO: That's the last thing he wanted. Now, relieve me, General or God damn it, sit down, sir.

[*Furious,* GENERAL EVANS *does neither. He glares at the* CO, *and strides out of the room. The* CO *continues.*]

CO: Captain Martin!

MARTIN: Yes, sir.

CO: Begin!

[*Lights go down, then up on the small stage. Music is heard: the General's electronic* Liebestod, *composed for this play by the American composer Paul Earls. It mixes distorted Wagner with ominous, vibrating pulses of electronic sound.*

At rear, curtains behind the Officers' Club bandstand part, revealing the GENERAL *and* HIS WIFE, *in a bright spotlight, wearing masks and gowns similar to those worn Halloween night. They are two dancers, male and female, from Special Services, impersonating the General and his wife, whose names will be used from here on.*

Slowly, these two figures move forward, to the music, hand in hand. They look out over everyone seated before them, in lowered light, staring up at them. They look at each other. They embrace. The tortured Liebestod *soars. They part, stand staring down at all the people, hand in hand.*

They are a staggering sight. Their masks are very powerful. His, the face of a suffering demon; hers, the exquisite face of a beautiful Japanese Noh play woman. Their gowns, homemade, follow the shape of Japanese kimonos, but they have bright gouts of red cloth sewed on the skirts, like smears of blood. The GENERAL *carries a modern, professional bow and arrow, and his Army automatic pistol in its holster.*

They stand staring at everyone. The Liebestod *fades down, the reverberating pulses remain.*]

BATES: The battles now are over,
the thunder of hoofbeats
and the iron clash of arms.

MISS NOMURA: But the sky is lit
by the fires of war.
The smell of death infects the
world,
and blood rains down from heaven.

[*The* GENERAL *and* HIS WIFE, *hand in hand, move slowly forward.*]

BATES: And so the General has left the field,
and with his faithful wife
makes a sacred pilgrimage.

MISS NOMURA: Yes, to the dark Mountain of Death
he makes his final journey.

[*They journey. On their way, they stop and look up.*]

BATES: Evening falls.
Night comes upon them.
Birds fly up

and vanish
in the darkening sky.

[*The* GENERAL *and* HIS WIFE *arrive at a river.*]

MISS NOMURA: They have reached
the river Katusura.

BATES: They step into their boat,
To cross the deep waters.

[*The* GENERAL *now poles an imaginary boat, while*
HIS WIFE *rides seated at its prow, looking down into the*
water.]

MISS NOMURA: And she remembered
when long ago
down these same rivers
once they sailed,
when he was young
and tall and gentle—

BATES: Like God. But now her rivers
stream with blood,
choked on bodies of the young,
his soldiers, dead in the war—

MISS NOMURA: And she sees, there, deep
in the currents far below,
under the floating bodies
of all the young soldiers,
far beneath their hanging arms
and drifting hair,
she sees her face
and his.

ROUNDHOUSE [*breaking in*]: That's from the *Iliad!* They'd
been reading Homer!

MOORE: Jesus, thanks for telling us! Somebody give him a gold star. We almost got enough talent around here to do *South Pacific* again.

[*Everybody hushes him, and listens, intently. The* DANCERS *move, as the* GENERAL *and* HIS WIFE, *on their journey.*]

BATES: And now they cross the deep waters,
      their boat touches the shore,
      and they have come
      to the Mountain of Death.

[*The* GENERAL *and* HIS WIFE *step out of their boat, and face a steep ascent.*]

MISS NOMURA: Torments all around us
      visions of men in white gowns
      slitting open the veins of the
          young
      pouring chemicals into them
      to make them like themselves

BATES: And to the great Warrior
      and his beautiful wife
      they turn and say

MISS NOMURA: You, too, will come to this
      you, too, will come to this

BATES: And then they see the worst—
      the young, their children,
      given whips and knives

MISS NOMURA: And torches and guns
      and taught to kill the helpless
      without mercy, none

> to soak young hands in blood
> and slander the innocent with
>   pride
> And then,
> at last—

BATES: They reach the top,
the end of their journey.

[*Silence except for reverberating pulses of the* Liebestod. *Slowly, while* BATES *and* MISS NOMURA *speak
their lines, the* GENERAL *and* HIS WIFE *turn to each
other.*]

THE GENERAL: We have come at last
to this fearful place.

HIS WIFE: Here on the top
of the Mountain of Death.

THE GENERAL: A grove of pines
and a bed of stones—

HIS WIFE: Where young lovers
come to die.

THE GENERAL: It is hard to imagine us here,
as a suicide of lovers.

HIS WIFE: For we are neither of us young
or crossed in love,
or badly treated by the world.

THE GENERAL: No, power was ours,
we had many victories
but now we are here—

HIS WIFE: As an offering to the Lord Buddha
and a sign to the world.
God will know why we do this!

THE GENERAL: He will not turn
        his great and shining face
        away from us!

HIS WIFE: No, he will see us
        strong and mature
        in the shadow of suicide.

THE GENERAL: From the grime of long deceit
        washed stainless
        here
        where the voices of nations
        all fade away,
        here we stand

HIS WIFE: A friend and a mother
        who throw away our world
        to follow our children
        and share their fate.

[*The* GENERAL *steps forward and raises one arm in a large and sweeping gesture.*]

THE GENERAL: O my country, farewell.
        You once were all the world to me.
        As best I could
        what you taught me
        I became,
        and served you far too well.
        I am yours no longer.

[HIS WIFE *kneels.*]

HIS WIFE: O gentle, shining, compassionate
        Buddha,
        before your beautiful face
        I met my young husband
        so many years ago.

Strengthen his hand
and show us the path,
the way to you!
Husband
do it now!

[*She lifts her face to him.*]

THE GENERAL: The knife may part the flesh
and miss the heart
and degrade this noble act.
No.

HIS WIFE: No. You must choose your bow
and your arrow tipped in steel
for which you are famous.

[*The* GENERAL *notches a steel-tipped arrow onto the string of his bow, but does not raise it.*]

THE GENERAL: But now it is time to kill you.
My knees grow weak.
For you are the body of the woman
I have loved all my life
and I shake with love
until you cry out!

HIS WIFE: Kill me! Kill me!
I will wait for you in heaven,
my noble husband!

[*He begins to draw the bow. Then, quite suddenly, he sees something coming toward them, and he quickly lowers it.*]

THE GENERAL: Wife! Look!
There!

Our child! My boy!
Our son!

HIS WIFE: He has come to us!
He has come to meet us
and lead us
into paradise!

[COLONEL MOORE *goes to the table hiding items in evidence and takes up the infant's toilet seat. He begins to clap the toilet seat up and down.*]

CO: That's Captain Stretch? There?

MARTIN: Yes, sir. That's Stretch, right there.

CO: What the hell was he doing?

MOORE: I'll show you what he was doing! This! [*He claps the toilet seat up and down.*] This! Just like this!

MARTIN: He wore a child's Halloween mask and he carried a toilet seat from a child's potty.

MOORE: And he danced and pranced all around them, calling them *Ma-ma* and *Da-da* and playing with this thing, and then—then he put it down on the floor and sat on it, and took a make-believe crap right there in front of them, and all over their ridiculous play.

MARTIN: That's right, sir. Saturday night, Stretch thought that was funny!

MISS NOMURA [*passionately*]: And so did you! So did you all!

CO: Well, did they laugh?

MARTIN: Yes, sir. When Stretch did his act, and started that stuff, the place came down. Everybody thought

99

that was finally the point of the whole thing. A dirty joke. Everybody was laughing, hard.

MOORE: Right! Good, healthy, wholesome American laughter!

MISS NOMURA: And I could see the tears running down from inside their masks!

CO: What? Is that where—

MARTIN: Yes, sir! With everybody laughing at them.

MOORE: Yes, everybody *was* laughing. And to tell you the truth, it's funny all over again, right up to the grisly end. Captain Stretch was the only one out there with any sense! Just wait until you figure out what was *really* going on! What they *really* died for!

MISS NOMURA [*passionately*]: They died for beauty, truth and love! For the cause of love and truth and beauty!

MOORE: Nuts, honey! Nuts!

ROUNDHOUSE [*laughing*]: Oh, no tragedy, no tragedy! Just bad, sloppy, cheap, shabby, undependable, fraudulent, fly-by-night American goods, that's all! Michael wanted to die in tragedy, but turned into farce! An American farce!

MOORE: Farce, was it! Farce, my royal ass! Look! Look here! What do you think these things are! [*He goes to the four gilded chairs, and drags out one with the* RE-SERVED *sign pinned onto it.*] Here! RESERVED! For who? When do you think he first got the idea for this God-awful mess, anyhow? September 25th, that's when. And who gave it to him? The man who didn't come, but who damn near did, and who almost sat right here in this chair Saturday night! The man that lunatic General pretended *had* come! The President of the United States, that's who! The General wanted either to kill himself in front of the whole world, by doing it in the lap of the Commander in Chief, or worse! Because what we really might have had here was not a public suicide at all, but a Presidential assassination!

LUCY LAKE: No, wait. That's not what you mean.

MOORE: Yes, I mean it! [*He glares at* LUCY LAKE, *who is moving to center.*] The President of the United States, Lucy Lake! Shot to death, right here!

LUCY LAKE [*at center*]: No, no. That child. Yoshida Robinson. The bequest to the orphanage. Losing children —Oh. I know what he was going to do. And what he meant us to discover. [*She reconstructs where everyone was.*] The President?

MOORE: There! Right there!

LUCY LAKE: The General? And the child would have come running—

MRS. BATES: There!

[*She runs to the spot where* YOSHI *would have entered. The ballroom* DANCERS *move into the places where the* GENERAL *and* HIS WIFE *stood waiting for the child. The* GENERAL *and* HIS WIFE *are standing right in front of the President's chair.*]

LUCY LAKE: The General was going to kill the child. He was going to kill an Oriental-American orphan boy, and throw his blood on the President of the United States. And then kill his wife, and himself. That would have been specific. That was *the* poem.

101

[*A shocked silence. Then, eruption.* MRS. BATES, *outraged by* LUCY LAKE'*s deduction, screams at her.*]

MRS. BATES: No! No! He wouldn't have never done that! He was a good man! A good man!

[*Improvisation: everyone arguing, passionately and loudly with everyone else about the* GENERAL, *each interpreting the love suicide from his own experience, and attacking those opposed.* COLONEL MOORE *is the loudest, and their arguments mix in with his.*]

MOORE [*with everyone else arguing at the same time*]: Oh, no, no! He was a baby, an overgrown American Boy Scout, and they're the terrors of the earth! [*To* LUCY LAKE] And don't you hand me any more of this shit about love and poetry and child sacrifice, or anything like that! He wanted center stage of the world, like a God-damned baby! Captain Stretch, with his kid's potty seat, was right! He was a baby, a God-damned Boy Scout baby!

[*Rage, chaos. The* CO *stands up and takes over briskly.*]

CO: That will do! This inquiry is not finished. We interrupted several testimonies. Judy.

[*His daughter steps forward. With increasing difficulty, she reads her letter from the General's wife.*]

MISS BORDEN [*reading*]: "My dear Judy, My husband and I are so sorry we were rude to you this summer about American history. It may be that your long-ago Senator was the good man you think him, and a cure for all our ills. I don't know. But I do know that your love of our history is good, and you will find again what is brave, and young, and good in the soul of our country. I pray

God give you the American life you seek. It is there, and you will find it. Aloha." [*She steps back, crying.*]

CO: Sergeant Bates. You have a message to me from the General, to be read aloud at the end of this inquiry. Read it.

[BATES *steps forward, opens the envelope he has kept with him throughout the inquiry and reads it aloud.*]

BATES [*reading*]: "General: If you have conducted my inquiry, I thank you. It represents a battle I lost, and the end of my lifelong dream of serving my country. My maneuvers here, many of them devious, may suggest the forces that defeated me. I hope so. I leave you to decide what duty to our country, and to ourselves, finally is. It was a choice I chose not to make. I wish you good luck, good conscience, and good-by."

[*The* CO *reaches out and takes the message.* BATES *steps back.*]

CO: Medical report.

[MAJOR CASSIDY *steps forward and reads his report, coldly and dispassionately.*]

CASSIDY: The General's wife died from the intrusion, into her throat, of a steel-tipped archer's arrow, shot from a sixty-pound bow. It severed the right carotid artery. She herself took the arrow in both hands, wrenched it back and forth in her throat. The General then took off his mask, drew his Army automatic, placed it against his ear, and pulled the trigger. The force of the explosion, at that range, removed the entire cranial vault. He literally blew out his brains, and both deaths were suicide. [*He steps back.*]

103

[*Silence. The telephone on the* CO's *desk rings, harshly. They all stare at it. The* CO *picks it up.*]

CO: Yes? [*Pause*] I understand. [*He hangs up.*] This inquiry is over. I have been relieved of this command. [*To* CAPTAIN MARTIN] All this material is now classified information. You will forward it at once to Army Headquarters in Washington, for proper review, at the proper time, under the Uniform Code of Military Justice. I thank you all very much. Good afternoon. [*He walks out.*]

[*Pulses of the* GENERAL's Liebestod *are heard. Stunned, the people drift out of the ballroom. The* DANCERS *are the last to go. They take off the masks, and set them down on the bandstand, by the bow and arrow, the two faces leaning against each other, upright. They exit. The lights fade, very slowly, on the staring masks of the* GENERAL *and* HIS WIFE, *ghosts in the falling darkness.*]

Epilogue

In his car, driven alone from Schofield Barracks to Pacific Army Headquarters at Fort Shafter, General Borden, with great concentration, wrote the following:

> I was not relieved of my command until the inquiry I conducted was terminated. I therefore submit my own report and my own conclusions.
>
> The General and his wife died for psychological reasons unknown, and impossible to discover. The only discovery the inquiry made was that they meant their deaths to be a sort of gesture, signifying something more than suicide. That much is certain.
>
> But the gesture was very complex. It consisted not only of the suicide, but also of the inquiry into the causes of that suicide. Each person called to it, including myself, the General called from varying experiences in his own life, and from widely differing backgrounds in American life.
>
> For Colonel Moore, a devout pragmatist, whose abilities the General valued highly, his suicide was the hysterical act of a collapsing fraud. From his viewpoint, the General was a sort of dangerous, overgrown American Boy Scout, deranged by a frightening world catching up with him. Which he could not tolerate, and fled.
>
> For Katherine Nomura, an American citizen of Japanese ancestry, their love suicide was perfectly acceptable. It was a pure and noble act, an honorable redemption from the tangles of worldly illusion, and a great achievement.

Let it be noted that the General took great pains to find her, and to use her in their play.

For Sergeant Major Ruggles, added to his list probably late Saturday afternoon, following their interview, the General's self-destruction was the act of a man unable to face the fact that he was a killer, which in Sergeant Major Ruggles' belief is an honorable part of man's estate. Let the General's written admiration of him also be noted.

For Lieutenant General Evans, with whom the General shared not only thirty years of friendship and Army service, but also the loss in battle of a beloved son, they were both casualties of war. Losses, which no matter how tragic, must never undermine the self-reliance of the nation in an unpredictable world, as embodied in dedicated and intelligent armed forces. And the General did send for him.

For Edward Roundhouse, it was a religious conversion. Turning ironically upon the General's early concern for sensitive soldiers, upon the shock of his soldier-trained mugging on the streets of New York, and on the ancient eloquence of a Greek poem, which had also disturbed another suicide, a dedicated American public servant. The conversion, familiar in religious history, was Warrior into Saint, with sainthood achieved by, not only the admission, but also the total and complete embrace of a guilt few others would ever admit existed. But whose death, ironically again, became a grotesque farce, as was indeed the destruction of Edward Roundhouse's own career in American education. He, too, was called to the inquiry, and by his name the General had written, "an old friend."

For Private Bowers and Warrant Officer LeVandre, the act was beyond comprehension. Yet each functioned. LeVandre supplied modernized, Western love-death music, to balance their Japanese suicide play, and Bowers wrote and released a clear account of the facts of the event before anyone could stop him. By orders from the General.

For Lucy Lake, a poet, the love suicide was itself a poem, taken from classical Japanese theatre, but laced throughout with the guilt of American ambition in this present era, ambition leading the General to a subconscious urge to sacrifice his own son, which, in his life, he accomplished. To which poem, in Miss Lake's opinion, as a recognition of removed, detached and inhuman decisions that slaughter present, specific human children, the General planned to add the staggering and revolting specific item of the murder of an Oriental-American orphan child before the President of the United States.

For Mrs. Bates, a terrible dilemma. Anguish for those who had redeemed her, but who were themselves then destroyed, by their discovery of the same abject shallow confusions of American reality, against which they were too dedicated, too decent, and, finally, too fragile to stand, and survive. And who, unlike Mrs. Bates, met no one who could come into their lives to help them. And let Lorna Ann Bates's great anger be noted, anger and frustration, because she was certain none of us could ever comprehend the shock of that discovery of theirs, and their suffering from it, as she alone could. And no child murder.

For her husband, Sergeant Bates, a simple, slow grief, asking no questions.

For Major Cassidy, the professional objectivity of a doctor, which allowed no consideration that the General was of unsound mind.

For Judith Borden, my daughter, the loss of an understanding woman, an Army brat once herself, who nevertheless encouraged my daughter's original research into past history involving shameful American acts.

For myself, Commanding Officer of Schofield Barracks for this past day and a half, this:

Exactly why the General and his wife chose suicide, even given their deep involvement with past Japanese culture, I myself cannot understand. That never, in my judgment, is a solution to anything. I must simply think about it for a long time, and about whatever bearing it may have on my duty as an American soldier. That, rather than judgment, is what he wanted from me.

But what I do understand is military strategy. And while my own relationship with the General was one of affable but strict formality, as befits commanding and executive officers, I was very much aware of the full extent of his strategic resourcefulness.

If, in the testimonies given during the inquiry, attention is paid to particular dates of most of the events described, it will, I believe, be evident that what the General mounted was not only a love suicide, but also a military campaign of considerable ambition.

First, no blood was shed but their own. The child would certainly never have been allowed to join them on that dance floor. A bewildered little boy, faced by a masked man with a bow and arrow, armed with a knife, would have been instantly defended, by all the people there. Indeed, the child was never sent in at all. Yoshida Robinson was protected by Mrs. Bates herself, as the General no doubt knew would be the case. Second, their Japanese love-suicide play was written *after* the President's visit to Hawaii was canceled. Those American antique armchairs, the testimony that the President might have come, and the poetic presence of Lucy Lake were quite enough to insure that in his agonies he had considered such a thing, that such a terrible and awesome possibility would be raised. It was. And so the child was murdered and resurrected during the inquiry alone, with no pain and no bloodshed. And with no personal affront to the General's Commander in Chief, to whom, as long as he could live, he was loyal.

Now, finally and most crucially, the purpose of the inquiry. The General chose his Executive Officer to conduct it, an executive officer whose character he understood and relied upon. He was right again. But I conducted an inquiry that was not really a search for one cause of their suicide, which will never be found, but, I believe, for a quite different reason.

It was his battlefield, upon which he laid out opposing forces his death would bring into conflict. Each of us called represented armies within him, which defeated him, armed forces of American life he then sent into battle himself, each against the other, quite literally over his dead body.

His art was the cruel art of war. He was a soldier, not a poet or a philosopher, and he could not reconcile the forces, the choices of his life, that conquered him. What he could do was throw them at each other, in combat. Which might be victorious, and which defeated, he left us to determine, each for ourself, as we struggled with each other. It is a battle unique in military history.

And he achieved his objective. Private Bowers will no doubt write a book about it, when he returns to civilian life. Lucy Lake will write her poems, to be read everywhere. And if that is not enough, the stark brutality of the scandal, now in the possession of the public, will engender countless scandalous interviews.

One person, I see, I have forgotten. Captain Stretch, in his hospital bed with a temperature of a hundred and five. He was also called by the General to his inquiry. But that was before he played out his hideous joke on the dance floor. Captain Stretch, when his fevers leave him, has his own story to tell about the General and himself. I hope he, like the rest of us, will be allowed to tell it.

Given the General's strategy, I do not see what else can happen.

He then signed his name below what he had written: Thomas N. Borden, Brigadier General, U.S.A. And he read it all again, and wondered what he would do with it, what it would do with him, as his car rolled past the gates of Pacific Army Headquarters.

Democracy and Esther

From two novels by Henry Adams

CHARACTERS

ULYSSES S. GRANT, *President of the United States*

JULIA GRANT, *his wife*

BARON JACOBI, *Bulgarian Minister*

ESTHER DUDLEY, *photographer*

GEORGE STRONG, *geologist*

STEPHEN HAZARD, *priest*

MRS. SAMUEL BAKER, *lobbyist*

JOHN CARRINGTON, *artist*

MRS. MADELEINE LIGHTFOOT LEE, *widow from New York*

THE HON. SILAS P. RAITCLIFFE, *Senator from Illinois*

LYDIA DUDLEY, *spinster*

SERVANTS

TIME: The 1870's, toward the end of Grant's second administration

PLACE: Washington, D.C.

Act One: The Past

———————•—————————

[*Washington, D.C. in the 1870's. Across the back wall of the theatre, a painted montage of the American capital: the Potomac, Georgetown façades, Rock Creek Park, the arches and stained-glass windows of the Washington Cathedral, the face of the White House, the lawn at Mount Vernon. At the sides of the stage hang chandeliers, ornate windows and deeply sensuous draperies, but at stage center are a set of light and serviceable tables, chairs and couches, which can be quickly moved about into various skeletons of different rooms. Through the play flow quicksteps, schottisches, waltzes, hymns and marches: the vigorous direct music of the Republic. At times, the lights sweep across this montage to the rhythms of that music, giving to each change of scene a sense of the whole: the parlors, bandstands, open streets and seats of power, the many vistas of a growing city now buried one hundred years in the American past.*

The White House, a reception room. Lights come up brightly. A band plays "Hail to the Chief" with jaunty speed. Smiling only slightly, in his stiff, calm manner, PRESIDENT GRANT *enters. With him, smiling broadly, is his wife,* JULIA. *People applaud.*]

GRANT: Ladies and gentlemen, I thank you for coming. I hope you will have a pleasant time this afternoon. I mean to, and so does Julia. Refreshments will be served in the next room there immejetly afterward. Thank you very much.

[*Everyone applauds again. They form a line to shake hands with the* PRESIDENT *and his* LADY. *While they do, a small, dapper European gentleman of sixty, with a shiny black cane in his hand and an orchid in his buttonhole, smiles at us.*]

JACOBI: How do you do? When I write my memoirs, I am going to call them *Thirty Years in Washington*, or *The End of Jacobi, Bulgarian Minister.* I will show you how that happens and introduce you to this strange garden of an American capital. Are you fond of flowers? The climate here is perfect. In Washington, the most amazing things will bloom. [*He points to the receiving line, where* GRANT *is shaking hands with everyone.*] Ulysses Grant, the great general who won the war. Magnificent. In 1854, he was thrown out of the Army, an alcoholic. For the next eight years, he could not support his family. He was working in his father's store, as a clerk for fifty dollars a month, in 1861. Seven years later, he was President of the United States. You see what I mean.

[JULIA GRANT *waves to* JACOBI, *who waves back.*]

That is his wife, Julia Grant, hopelessly cross-eyed. When they moved into the White House, she was going to have a surgical operation, but the President stopped her. He told her he had loved her cross-eyed all these years, and didn't want her to change. You see what I mean.

[*A charming, vibrant girl in her middle twenties moves down from the receiving line.*]

JACOBI: Esther Dudley, who makes photographs with cameras. She is also the daughter of the Chief Justice of the United States. She is considered terribly bohemian, and her heart, you will be told, belongs to free thought, horses and Mathew Brady.

[*A plain, sturdy man in his early thirties moves after her, puts a hand on her arm and talks to her.*]

George Strong, geologist. Childhood friend, as devoted to Esther as to fossils and fishbones.

[*A second man, a very handsome clergyman, is brought down to* ESTHER *by* GEORGE STRONG, *and introduced to her.*]

This beauty is the Reverend Stephen Hazard. He has the luck to possess Washington's highest Episcopal pulpit, most thrilling voice and bluest eyes. He is going to ask Esther Dudley to photograph his north transept. She will.

[*They move away together. A woman in the crowd throws back her head and laughs, loudly.*]

Mrs. Samuel Baker, lobbyist. She has more influence in Congress than is good for anyone. You wouldn't think she would be successful, but she is.

[MRS. BAKER *laughs again. A man with desperate eyes comes to* JACOBI.]

CARRINGTON: All right. When are we going to see Mrs. Lee's Corot?

JACOBI: At her soiree this week. That's what she told me. Isn't that right?

CARRINGTON: Yes, it is. You'll be there, then?

JACOBI: Of course. Now tell me, how is your liver?

CARRINGTON: Rotten, thank you. But the painting is good. When are you coming to the cathedral?

JACOBI: Saturday morning?

CARRINGTON: Early?

JACOBI: By all means.

CARRINGTON: Good. You can pour my first drink of the day. I will see you then?

JACOBI: You will see me then.

[CARRINGTON *weaves back into the crowd, observant but shaky. He drinks steadily.*]

John Carrington, a dying cliché. Drunken painter from Virginia, all alone in a roomful of success. Say nothing against him.

[JACOBI *is approached by a very handsome woman in her early forties.*]

MRS. LEE: Baron Jacobi, I must hold you to your promise.

JACOBI: Promise, Mrs. Lee? Which one?

MRS. LEE: I told you I wanted to know Senator Raitcliffe. There he is.

JACOBI: This instant, madame, he shall be yours.

MRS. LEE: Thank you.

[JACOBI *waves to* SENATOR RAITCLIFFE, *who scowls at first, then, when he sees* MRS. LEE, *smiles ever so slightly and joins them, cautiously.*]

RAITCLIFFE: My compliments, sir.

JACOBI: And mine, sir. I will plant flowers this afternoon, Senator, to bloom in the spring. For this charming lady, who is Mrs. Madeleine Lightfoot Lee, newly arrived in Washington, I will implant one Late-blooming, Gold-banded American Lily. And for you, Senator Silas P. Raitcliffe, also of this city, one red-white-and-blue United States Bachelor's Button.

MRS. LEE: I thank you, Baron Jacobi, very much.

RAITCLIFFE: And I, sir, thank you also.

JACOBI: I am delirious with pleasure. You will excuse me. [*He leaves the widow and the Senator together.*]

MRS. LEE: I heard your speech yesterday, Senator Raitcliffe.

RAITCLIFFE: Did you, indeed, madam?

MRS. LEE: Indeed I did, sir, and I want to tell you I was impressed. It seemed to me masterful, Senator. Surely it will have a great effect?

RAITCLIFFE: Why, madam, I hope it will help in some measure to unite the party. That was its purpose.

MRS. LEE: May I confess something to you?

RAITCLIFFE: By all means.

MRS. LEE: When I left New York, everyone told me I would be shocked by the falling-off of political ability in Washington. I didn't believe them, and when I heard your speech, I knew I was right. Do you yourself think there is less ability in Congress now than formerly?

119

RAITCLIFFE: Well, there are different customs. Life is more complex.

MRS. LEE: Am I right in thinking you have a strong resemblance to Daniel Webster in your way of speaking? You come from the same region, do you not?

RAITCLIFFE: Well, as a matter of fact, we do. But I cannot assume the pretension, madam, of ranking myself with such an exalted personage.

MRS. LEE: You're too modest, Senator. Until you teach me better, I will consider your phrase "the tangled mass of isolated principles, the hair of the half-sleeping Giant of Party" quite equal to anything of Webster's. The force of your language, sir, makes me blush like a girl.

RAITCLIFFE: Why, madam—

MRS. LEE: And if you consider the memory of Clay, and Calhoun, even, not to mention vengeful Randolph—

RAITCLIFFE: Mrs. Lee, your grasp of American politics is—

MRS. LEE: —thank you—how can one help but admire the giants of today, men who must face their duties with no answers from the past— [*They move into the crowd.*]

[ESTHER *comes by, talking to* STRONG.]

ESTHER: Oh, George, stop it. I can't work in a church.

STRONG: And why not?

ESTHER: Because I'm a heathen. Can you imagine me there?

STRONG: I can imagine an architectural study. An essay in pictures.

ESTHER: I'd feel like an actress, pretending. I'd pack away my gear, develop my plates, and there wouldn't be anything there. I have other things to do.

STRONG [*gently*]: More portraits of your father? Of his house on M Street? Of his favorite rocking chair, his library, his garden, his stables? Esther, you've done nothing but nurse him for a solid year. You've got to do something else.

ESTHER: I know.

STRONG: Do you remember when we used to play hide and seek, and it came your turn to find me?

ESTHER: Yes.

STRONG: Sometimes I would wait and wait, crouched behind a bush or squashed down under the porch. No Esther. And then I would have to go and find you. And there you'd be, looking just the way you're looking right now, brooding over something, our game forgotten. I know that morbid streak in you, and that's why I asked Hazard to put you to work. It wasn't his idea at all.

ESTHER: You did, George? Why?

STRONG: So you can photograph transepts and arches and archangels and God Almighty, for all I care, and get your mind off your father. You must, Esther!

ESTHER: I know. But—

STRONG: What?

ESTHER: I can't stop waiting. For the end. It's not conceivable that next year he won't be where he is right now, waiting for me at home.

STRONG: Esther, that's morbid! You're a big girl now. Get your cameras and your pots and pans and make beautiful pictures. Do it!

ESTHER: Well, George—

STRONG: No, don't fret about it, *just do it!*

ESTHER [*smiling*]: Do *you* fret, George? About me?

STRONG: Of course not.

ESTHER: You have nothing but picks and rocks and chalk and plate glass in your head. Is that it?

STRONG: Absolutely.

ESTHER: You're right. I'll try.

STRONG: That's my girl!

ESTHER: Where's your preacher! Let's see what the gentleman has in mind!

[*They move into the crowd.* JACOBI *swings round again, this time with a very old lady. They stand watching* RAITCLIFFE *and* MRS. LEE, *who are across the room, deep in conversation.*]

LYDIA: Now, then, Jacobi. Who is that woman with the ring through Raitcliffe's nose? Mrs. Lee, I know, but what does that mean?

JACOBI: Fifth Avenue widow. Washington appetites. What do you think?

LYDIA: I think she has the looks. What's the background?

JACOBI: The Raymonds of Philadelphia. And her late husband was a northern branch of the Virginia Lees.

LYDIA: Well, that will certainly do. Has she set up camp?

JACOBI: Oh, yes. Charming house on H Street. Small evenings only, so far, but they expand next week. Would you be at all interested, Lydia?

LYDIA: Jacobi, you Bulgarian weasel, you know perfectly well I would. I'll bring Esther, and her young men.

JACOBI: Mrs. Lee will be delighted, I'm sure.

LYDIA: But you really must tell the woman she is underrating Silas Raitcliffe. She won't stuff and mount him without a fight.

JACOBI: I'll tell her.

LYDIA: Good. Now, then, the President has entrusted me with something very grave.

JACOBI: What?

LYDIA: A secret mission. [*Pause*] Want to know what it is?

JACOBI: Please.

LYDIA: I must change his wife's mind.

JACOBI: That shouldn't be difficult, if you can manage to find it.

LYDIA: You see my problem. Do tell Mrs. Lee I shall await her invitation with pleasure. Now where on earth is Julia Grant? Oh, yes. [*She totters into the crowd.*]

JACOBI: Lydia Dudley, Esther's aunt and the sister of Chief Justice Dudley. She is a spinster older than her country. Her father was a great favorite of General

Washington's, and so, as a little girl, was she. Oh, shall we listen to this?

[ESTHER *and* HAZARD *come round.*]

ESTHER: Well, you're an interesting man, but I must say you're a very odd priest. I hope you're not expecting miracles, Reverend Hazard.

HAZARD: Miss Dudley, reverends seldom do.

ESTHER: I work best with models, doing portraits.

HAZARD: Then use them.

ESTHER: What?

HAZARD: Why not? A Christian cathedral, Miss Dudley, does have people inside it, occasionally. You might find the right girl—one pretty enough—and catch her under John Carrington's Saint Cecelia.

ESTHER: You make that sound very easy. Finding saintly girls is not so simple.

HAZARD: The problem does not seem to me beyond all solution. I could find one now.

ESTHER: What?

[HAZARD *stares at her steadily. In spite of herself,* ESTHER *blushes.*]

ESTHER: Reverend Hazard, that's the most God-awful compliment in the whole history of flirting. You ought to be ashamed of yourself.

HAZARD: But I'm not. Just come to church in the morning, and we'll begin.

ESTHER: On *what*, may I ask?

HAZARD [*laughing*]: On photography. I'm really quite proper, I'm sorry to say. My brazen manners have innocent ulterior motives. Fun, flirting, a little work; they may help you through difficult days.

ESTHER: Oh. George told you?

HAZARD: Yes. I had no idea your father was so ill. May I tell you I have always considered him to be the finest man in this country?

ESTHER: Thank you.

HAZARD: When the time does come, if I can help you, let me. There are so many difficult details. I am used to them, and you are not. There is no greater strain than to stand for the first time in the face of eternity, as you will then. You will need help.

ESTHER: I will need endurance. Can you give me that?

HAZARD: That is just what you mustn't want, believe me. You will exhaust your strength, the last thing your father would want. I can do little for him, but I can be concerned about you. Will you rely on me?

ESTHER: Oh, well, let me think about Saint Cecelia first, may I?

HAZARD [*quickly*]: By all means.

[*They move into the crowd.* MRS. LEE *and* RAITCLIFFE *appear.* MRS. LEE *and* RAITCLIFFE *come around again.*]

RAITCLIFFE: —is in the Connecticut River Valley, if you recall.

MRS. LEE: So you are a New England Yankee, then, and not a native Midwestern Giant at all?

RAITCLIFFE: Not at all. But you mustn't say that when you hear me talking about my beloved Illinois, heartland of the Republic.

MRS. LEE [*laughing*]: I promise.

RAITCLIFFE: Thank you. Yes, I received a classical education at the Valley Academy near my home. Everything else I learned by myself, in the arena. That education, Mrs. Lee, has little symmetry, but a great deal of substance.

MRS. LEE: Since everyone agrees you are the ablest man in Congress, I must believe you. And even in very polished circles, true ability speaks for itself. An American senator, Senator, after all is said and done, represents a sovereign state. Illinois, if I am not mistaken, is as large as England.

RAITCLIFFE: You are not mistaken, madam.

MRS. LEE: What position, then, surpasses that of an American senator? An American president, nothing less. And do not, I beg you, speak to me of classical education. When my husband died five years ago, I resorted in my boredom to desperate measures. I read philosophy in German, and nothing is more desperate than that. The more I read, the more my heart sank as I saw so much culture leading to so little pleasure. I plunged into practical life: visited prisons, inspected hospitals and poorhouses. I wallowed in the correction of vice until I had lost all my virtue. I turned to religion. But, I was unable to imagine all those busy American Christians claiming *me* as their prophet. What's the matter?

126

RAITCLIFFE: Your flow of oratory, madam, is amazing.

MRS. LEE: You see why I admired your speech. Shall I powder my face and shut my mouth?

RAITCLIFFE: Good heavens, no. I wish we had you in the Senate. Do go on. I am yours, entirely.

MRS. LEE: Are you, really? Well, good. What, then, to seek, and what to sacrifice myself for? High ideals? Passion for the lofty and the pure? No. I rebelled. I lost my sense of duty. As far as I was concerned, all the criminals in the country could rise up in their glory and manage every railway on the continent; what, frankly, did I care? If the heathen refuse to be converted, should I, a woman, run after them with the sword and the stake? Nonsense. Well, what then? My friends from Boston said: "Go about in brilliant society," meaning, of course, go about in Boston. Yet I found Boston society hardly less calcified than my own. What to do? It was absurd to stay in New York, spending money; vulgar to live in two houses when you only needed one, among a wilderness of men and women as monotonous as the stones of the mansions they inhabit.

RAITCLIFFE: I believe a journey to Europe is generally an accepted answer. You found no excitement there?

MRS. LEE: I found in Europe a beautiful little Corot landscape, and that is all. I brought it back with me. You must see it one day.

RAITCLIFFE: I hope I will.

MRS. LEE: So do I. But finally, when Europe was exhausted, and I was exhausted, and there was nothing fashionable left to do, I found myself alone with my country. I came to admit that I was an American woman to the tips of my fingers. Why, then, should I not take all that American life has to offer, good or bad? And the center, the pulse of American life, was not in New York, but here, in Washington. And so here I am. I am an American woman and I want to know more about my country. Does that seem to you presumptuous, and unfeminine, Senator?

RAITCLIFFE: On the contrary, it seems to me womanly beyond description.

MRS. LEE: Well, I am learning. Before I came to Washington, my notion of a legislative body was vague, to say the least. It floated about between my experience at church on one end and at the opera on the other. I assumed all those speeches had some purpose, but I never worried myself about what that purpose might be.

RAITCLIFFE: That is a very common conception of Congress, madam. Many Congressmen share it.

MRS. LEE [*laughing*]: Now, that's charming, Senator. Why do you repress that wit? I find it beguiling. And surely you must have a sense of humor to exist in politics at all. Tell me about that.

[*They swing around into the crowd.* LYDIA DUDLEY *and* JULIA GRANT: JULIA *very dubious about what* LYDIA *is suggesting to her*]

JULIA: But I can't do that. I can't do that. I just don't see how I can do anything like that at all.

LYDIA: Just send the invitation with a note saying it was misplaced.

JULIA: But that would be a lie.

LYDIA: Yes, I know, my dear, but under the circumstances, don't you think it would be justified?

JULIA: I am married to the President of the United States. I don't have to go around telling lies to the wife of some Spanish Ambassador.

LYDIA: Then send the invitation and say nothing.

JULIA: That is just impossible. I'm not going to have the woman in my house.

LYDIA: But—

JULIA: Not that I hold one thing against her personally. I have never met the creature. It's the principle of it. The whole thing's impossible.

LYDIA: But, my dear Mrs. Grant, relations with Spain are so very delicate. Don't you think your husband needs your diplomatic help at a ticklish moment?

JULIA: Yes, of course. But you tell me how I can invite her to sit at my table, under my roof. It is plain knowledge that the woman lived with her husband *before* they were married. I can't have that come walking into the White House, can I?

LYDIA: If war with Spain is a consideration, Mrs. Grant, I really do think you might shave that principle down just a bit. Let me do it for you. Would that be agreeable?

JULIA: You mean I won't have to do it myself?

LYDIA: I will take your invitation to her by hand, this afternoon. We must try to allow other people their own codes of behavior, my dear, as difficult as that sometimes seems to us.

JULIA: Yes, but the idea of a woman coming in here who's lived with a man without being married to him—

LYDIA: But, my dear Mrs. Grant, they are *married now!*

JULIA: But they *weren't then!* I tell you it's unheard of! But I'll rely on you, Miss Dudley. Go ahead and invite her. I'll rely on you.

[CARRINGTON *and* JACOBI *stroll by, watching* RAIT-CLIFFE *and* MRS. LEE.]

CARRINGTON: Jacobi, she's too decent a woman to squander herself on that Prairie Giant. What a cold fraud that man is. Look at him, pretending to flop about at her feet with the hook in his mouth, like a great big flounder.

JACOBI: I do not think he is pretending as much as you say. And I was not aware, *mon ami,* that you had such strong regard for the charming Mrs. Lee.

CARRINGTON: Oh, yes.

JACOBI: When did you meet her, by the way?

CARRINGTON: Some years ago. I knew her husband some years ago.

JACOBI: Ah. I see.

[MRS. SAMUEL BAKER *swoops down on them, with designs on* CARRINGTON.]

MRS. BAKER: Oh, those hands! Those hands! John Carrington, you wonderful man, I just adore those beautiful pictures you paint with those hands.

CARRINGTON: Thank you, Mrs. Baker. Do you know Baron Jacobi?

MRS. BAKER: How are you? Wonderful to see you.

JACOBI: Charmed.

MRS. BAKER: I mean, John Carrington, you are just going to tell me all about your Last Judgment, and how you thought that whole idea up, having our Lord and Saviour there judging all the world, with those beautiful saints and terrible sinners; why, the things you have them doing right there on the church wall with those tiny little robes and dresses, well, it's thrilling anyway, all of it, and shows you are a man of such character. And those hands. Oh, those hands.

[*She drags* CARRINGTON *off.* ESTHER, STRONG *and* HAZARD *come around, all three in a very pleasant mood. There is a marked change in* ESTHER.]

ESTHER: Last night, of all things in the world, I dreamed that Nathaniel Hawthorne came into my bedroom.

HAZARD: What did he want?

ESTHER: The same thing you do, both of you. The very same thing.

HAZARD [*chuckling*]: Miss Dudley, if you talk like this to casual gentlemen at White House receptions, what do you say to patriotic ghosts in your bedroom?

ESTHER: The same thing I say to casual gentlemen at the White House. I lack your confidence. Not only in writing books and photographing cathedral walls, but in everything else, too.

STRONG: And how did the ghost of Hawthorne reply to that?

ESTHER: Just like you would, George. He got angry.

131

HAZARD: Are ghosts, then, upset when the living lack confidence?

ESTHER: Hawthorne was. My confusion annoyed him dreadfully. You should have seen him, in his great black wool coat, storming about my bedroom, with lightning flashing outside my window and thunder crashing through the sky. It was very dramatic.

STRONG: Did he frighten you?

ESTHER: Yes, but not enough. That's the trouble. I can't be frightened into confidence any more than I can be persuaded into it. Tell him about Hawthorne and me, George.

STRONG: That's all nonsense.

ESTHER: I wish it was. You see, Reverend Hazard, my father named me for one of Nathaniel Hawthorne's heroines. Esther Dudley, a keeper of the flame. Do you remember her?

HAZARD: Well, vaguely. I confess I am not overwhelmed by a passion for Hawthorne.

ESTHER: Neither am I. He gives me a headache. Nevertheless, I am named for his heroine.

HAZARD: And what was she like?

ESTHER: Do you really want to know?

HAZARD: Yes, I really do.

ESTHER: I wouldn't want to bore you.

HAZARD: That would be impossible.

ESTHER: Are you quite sure?

STRONG [*disgusted*]: Ladies and gentlemen, please!

ESTHER: Esther Dudley, for whom I was named, was a faithful keeper of the flame, but it turned out to be the wrong flame, you see. In Hawthorne's story, Esther Dudley was the housekeeper who would not leave the English Governor's mansion after the war. There she stayed, sweeping the floors, polishing the silver, and would not believe a revolution had come.

HAZARD: I think that's charming.

ESTHER: No, not really. For there she died, all alone. A curious antique, faithful to a vanquished King. She did not have very much confidence in the future, you see, and neither do I.

STRONG: Esther, what rot!

ESTHER: Oh, yes, I'm disgraceful! I let everyone down! I am supposed to be this optimistic sprout of an American girl, all bosom, giggles and womb! Instead, I run about with camera acids and collodion pans, and everyone says, how bohemian. There goes the daughter of the Chief Justice, taking pictures of the past, riding horses, challenging men. But I'm not very bohemian, either, because I go home very quickly, and stay there quietly with my father, and with him speak of things no one else will even admit exist.

HAZARD: Such as?

ESTHER: How much the war changed us all. That something was annulled, canceled out. I talk a great deal, once I start. Do you mind?

HAZARD: Miss Dudley, I'm a preacher. So do I. Go right ahead.

ESTHER: My skeptical and judicial father, Reverend Hazard, believed in the past, because in his day there wasn't any. Give me warmth! he would say. Some kind of honor and romance, in the name of God, to soften this brutal continent! And so he, and Hawthorne and their friends, created a past that never existed, and a future that is, at best, obscure. And they bound their children to those American visions like slaves to mill wheels. He created his own Esther Dudley: me. That was all wonderful, but now, from his sickbed, he holds Esther Dudley's hand, looks into the future, where she must live without him, and tells her point-blank he was wrong. They were all wrong. Nothing new was done. Nothing new will happen. Only law, and war.

STRONG: Esther! Your father has faith and courage, and so do you!

ESTHER: Oh, do I? No, George, I have become very literal, and frightened. When I go out with my cameras, it isn't in search of anything grand like faith or courage. No great American visions; just some little flat picture of a noun, some little person or thing, plain as a board. No greatness, no majesty, no sweep, if you please, just true. Something small, plain and true, so I will know it was really there, and wasn't a lie, or a vision, or a bad dream. That's what the country is now, my father says. With war and progress, you have to photograph it to believe it. Like Mathew Brady. Reverend Hazard, my father doesn't believe in his country any longer. He hates it. Where does that leave Esther Dudley?

HAZARD [gently]: Searching, perhaps, for something else to believe in.

134

ESTHER: Oh, dear. Gilded Episcopal melodrama. Faith, and happiness. Will she ever find it?

HAZARD: Laugh all you please, but it isn't melodrama; it's reality. And my answer is yes! I think she will!

STRONG: And so do I!

ESTHER: You casual gentlemen! Such confidence! You will believe in absolutely anything, if you think it worth while. Religion. Science. Progress. National Destiny. No matter what, if it seems to work, you will believe in it, and call it absolute, the truth. Well, that's all right perhaps for confident gentlemen, but what about me? Here I am, a spinster rapidly aging, Hawthorne raging in my dreams, addicted to small flat truth. I know it renders me repulsive and will no doubt corrupt me into bitchery, but what's the answer? What's the cure? Who can teach me? Gentlemen?

STRONG: Esther! Truth isn't a disease, like a fungus! It's a pursuit! It's fun, more exciting than you can possibly imagine! If you don't believe me, just take one look at my new book on fossil batrachians.

ESTHER: No, George. I don't need to face the origins of life, or come to a decision about the creation of the world. Small truth. Tiny things. What should a little girl see? Where should a little girl stand? What do you tell your parishioners, Reverend Hazard?

HAZARD: I tell them to stand where they please, and look about where they wish, and sooner or later their doubts will be cured. As yours will, in time.

ESTHER: By what medicine? Tell me!

HAZARD: By life. You will see.

ESTHER: Oh, please! All life will do is ruin my complexion and addle my wits so it doesn't matter what I believe. I know that well enough. It's what finally happened to Esther Dudley, after all. But—do you both really think there might be *some* hope for me? Reverend Hazard? George? Gentlemen?

STRONG: There must be, Esther, for you.

HAZARD: No must be about it. There is!

ESTHER: And so, if I read about your fossil batrachians, George, and if I photograph your north transept, Reverend Hazard, then perhaps I may be saved after all. And let someone else be Esther Dudley. That's very appealing.

[*They move away.* MRS. LEE *and* RAITCLIFFE *swing by again.*]

RAITCLIFFE: —and so I put myself forward, and did my dance for the party, but the President, with his enormous popularity, had picked out the music long before.

MRS. LEE: But will you always sacrifice yourself that way? Surely not forever.

RAITCLIFFE: It is no sacrifice, madam, to serve one's party.

MRS. LEE: And have your never, not even once, refused to go along with your party?

RAITCLIFFE: Never.

MRS. LEE: Nothing, then, is more powerful than faithfulness to the party?

RAITCLIFFE: Nothing.

MRS. LEE: What about faithfulness to the country?

RAITCLIFFE: They are the same thing, madam. The very same thing. My dear Mrs. Lee, I came to this reception out of duty, but I have stayed for pleasure. May I tell you how much I have enjoyed our little talk?

MRS. LEE: You may.

RAITCLIFFE: And that I look forward to another in the near future?

MRS. LEE: You may.

RAITCLIFFE: Then shall I call upon you?

MRS. LEE: Do.

RAITCLIFFE: And you are laughing at me again. Have pity. A widower forgets how to manage these materials. Help me.

MRS. LEE: I am always at home on Sunday evenings. How is that?

RAITCLIFFE: Just right. Good afternoon, Mrs. Lee.

MRS. LEE: Good afternoon, Senator Raitcliffe.

[*A band strikes up outside.* PRESIDENT GRANT *and* JULIA *step to the center of the room and address their guests.*]

GRANT: Ladies and gentlemen, we thank you for coming. I certainly had a nice time, and so did Julia.

JULIA: I sure did.

GRANT: We hope to see you all again soon. Thank you very much.

[GRANT *and* JULIA *leave, and everyone else follows. Outside, the band is playing "Hail to the Chief," and*

137

for a moment the stage is empty; then, in her coat,.
MRS. LEE *appears. She looks about, stands very quiet
and still, involved with her thoughts and the room she
is in.* JACOBI *appears and speaks softly to us.*]

JACOBI: Have you ever known passengers on ocean liners
who cannot rest until they go down into the engine
room to talk to the engineer? Who must see with their
own eyes the action of pistons, and touch with their
own hands the wheel of the ship?

[MRS. LEE, *brooding, exits very slowly.*]

JACOBI: She is in love again. Not with a senator, or a city,
or a future, or even a country, but with power. With
the clashing interests of forty million American people,
with the force of American will, with the rage of American government. It is American power, now, that will
rouse her female flesh, and ravish her!

["*Hail to the Chief*" *plays outside. Then, different
music: gay party songs. A change of light and furni-
ture, and the scene is* MRS. MADELEINE LIGHTFOOT
LEE's *Washington parlor, where an expanded soiree is
very much in progress. Festive voices indicate all is well
in adjoining rooms.* SENATOR RAITCLIFFE's *laugh
rings out freely, and pleasantly. Enter* CARRINGTON,
*carrying a glass dark with whiskey. After him comes
LYDIA DUDLEY.*]

LYDIA: Now, John, behave yourself. You can't talk to a
senator like that. And please, either stop drinking or
blot yourself to sleep.

CARRINGTON: I'll set his boardinghouse on fire. I'll burn
his Illinois state flag.

LYDIA: Mrs. Lee knows what she is about.

CARRINGTON: But she's no match for him. That man's a monster!

LYDIA: He's the most able man in Washington public life, and everybody knows it, including you. That Madeleine Lee will accept the first public man of the day is not surprising. That the first public man of the day will be delighted to have a fashionable and intelligent wife, with forty or fifty thousand a year, is not surprising, either. He may be from Peoria, Illinois, but he isn't a Mongoloid waterhead.

[*Enter* JACOBI]

JACOBI: Do I hear the rustle of soft whispers, and the click of knives? May I come in, and bring my poisoned cup?

LYDIA: Jacobi, you ugly man. If you are here to slander with spiteful rumors people far better than yourself, then tell us all you know.

[*Music. Chatter and the swirl of society.* MRS. LEE *and* RAITCLIFFE *move down front.*]

RAITCLIFFE: Will you come to the Senate tomorrow? With you for a critic I will speak a great deal better.

MRS. LEE: Am I such a friendly critic, then? Doesn't that defeat the purpose?

RAITCLIFFE: Not at all. It is justice alone that I would ever expect from you.

MRS. LEE: But what good does all the speechmaking actually do? Are you any nearer the end of your problems because of all your speeches?

139

RAITCLIFFE: I don't know yet. The trouble right now, you know, is the President. He thinks we are intriguing to tie up his hands, and so he schemes away his days to tie up ours, making foolish appointments, without taking advice. Like that idiot Mark Richmond, who made all the noise about reform of the Civil Service last week. That kind of man. Grant likes him because he knows all about horses. And dislikes Moteley, the best civil servant in the country, because he parts his hair in the middle and wears a monocle. Did you hear my response to Richmond?

MRS. LEE: I did, and it was brutal. I should think the man would hate you forever.

RAITCLIFFE: No, no. He'll be a little sore, that's all. Yet what drivel.

MRS. LEE: But is reform really so impossible as you say? Is it really quite hopeless?

RAITCLIFFE: Reform such as that numbskull Richmond advocates is hopeless, yes.

[*A few others have stopped talking and are listening to them.*]

MRS. LEE: But surely something must be done to check corruption. Forgive me, I know I may sound like a fool, but are we to live forever at the mercy of financial thieves and political bullies? Is respectable government impossible, after all, in American democracy?

JACOBI: What is that you say, Mrs. Lee? What is that about corruption?

[*Everyone gathers around and closes in.* MRS. LEE *stands her ground bravely.*]

MRS. LEE: I am asking Senator Raitcliffe what will happen to this country if present corruption goes unchecked?

JACOBI: And may I very respectfully venture to ask permission to hear the Senator's reply?

RAITCLIFFE: You may, sir. My reply is that no representative government can ever be much better or much worse than the society it represents. Purify society, and you purify government. But try to purify the government by artificial means, and you're a child, crying for the moon and the stars, which you will never possess. You only confuse your party, and make things worse.

MRS. LEE: What do you say to that, Baron Jacobi?

JACOBI: I congratulate the Senator on a statesmanlike reply.

MRS. LEE: But that itself is only statesmanlike. Senator Raitcliffe said what he thought. Why don't you?

JACOBI: Perhaps I will.

LYDIA: Go ahead, Jacobi. Why not?

MRS. LEE: Yes, why not? Speak up, please. I am only a crude socialite from New York City. I want to hear some answers.

CARRINGTON: Give them to her, Jacobi. The lady is waiting.

JACOBI: Oh, what good is any reply or any conclusion of mine? You won't listen. You Americans believe yourselves to be excepted from the operation of general laws. You care nothing for experience, none of you. I

have lived for seventy years, and much of it in the absolute middle of corruption. I am corrupt myself: a perverse, wicked, prejudiced, immoral old European
diplomat, just like they say, only I have the courage to
admit it, and you do not. Rome, Paris, Vienna, Peters-
burg, London, all are corrupt; only Washington is
pure! Well, let me tell you that in my life I've found no
society with all the elements of corruption like the
United States. The children in the streets are corrupt,
and know how to cheat me. The cities are all corrupt
and also the towns and the counties and the states'
legislatures and the judges. Everywhere men betray
trusts, both public and private, condemn the innocent,
steal money, pocket bribes, and run away with public
funds. Only in the Senate, you understand, do men take
no money! And now, in that same Senate, you declare
that your United States, and its great political parties,
the emerging leader of the world, should never learn
from corrupt and evil Europe. Well, quite right; where
corruption is concerned, the United States *needs* no
examples from wicked Europe! *Ah, le bon Dieu!* How I
wish I had another life ahead of me to live! If I did, do
you know where I would return? I would come back to
this city a hundred years from now, and I would be so
delightfully at home here then, much more so than I am
now. For I am most at home where I find the most corruption, and, *ma foi! parole d'honneur!* in one hundred
years the United States of America will be more corrupt than France under the Regent, than the Church
under Leo the Tenth, then Rome under Caligula!
[*There is a long pause.*] I am sorry to be vehement,
Mrs. Lee. But there is the conclusion for which I was
asked.

MRS. LEE [*shaken*]: Thank you very much.

RAITCLIFFE [*calmly*]: And one I see no reason to accept. It is commonplace strategy, sir, to acquire profound knowledge of all this vast nation in the armchair of a small embassy library, and parade it about at parties. Pardon me if I decline to overly excite myself. And if I go now to refresh my cup of tea.

MRS. BAKER [*reaching for his cup*]: Do let me, Senator Raitcliffe.

RAITCLIFFE: Thank you, madam. Why, Essy Baker, is it not?

MRS. BAKER: Yes, it is.

RAITCLIFFE: I knew your late husband very well. A most efficient worker, and a Christian gentleman. I am really very happy to see you here this evening.

[*They move into the other room.*]

JACOBI: Well, ladies and gentlemen, please excuse me and allow me to bang my head upon the floor.

LYDIA: Quite right. You ought to be ashamed of yourself, you debauched and jaded man. Consider yourself rebuked, and don't forget you are taking me home.

MRS. LEE: I did ask for it, didn't I?

LYDIA: You did, my dear, and you got it. But don't be distressed. Mr. Raitcliffe isn't.

MRS. LEE: Are you sure?

LYDIA: Perfectly. He is a very busy man. Operatic tirades don't faze him. I beg your pardon, Jacobi.

JACOBI: *De rien.*

MRS. LEE: But tell me, Miss Dudley, as I wander about here lost and forlorn, what *should* I think, really, about Baron Jacobi's speech? Are speeches made in Washington just for the fun of it, and is one allowed to say anything and mean nothing? Who and what is to be believed? Mr. Raitcliffe seems wise and honest. But is he telling the truth, or not?

LYDIA: He is much too busy, my dear, to consider that question at all. He's the best practical politician in Congress. Isn't it unfair to insist he be a crusader as well?

CARRINGTON: Lydia, wait a minute. He doesn't have to lead crusades, but he doesn't have to *obstruct* them, either. He talks virtue, but opposes the correction of vice.

LYDIA: That is simple shrewdness. You can't blame him if he attacks what he considers weak policy.

MRS. LEE [*plaintively*]: But who, then, is right? We can't all be right. Half our wise men tell us the world is hopelessly corrupt, the other half that it is slowly but surely being perfected. Both can't be right; they can't even be quite sane. I am a spoiled lady of society, but there is just one thing more I am going to have before I die. I am going to find out whether American Democracy is right or wrong, being perfected or being corrupted. I want to know whether to believe in Senator Raitcliffe, or not.

CARRINGTON: Well, let me tell you—

LYDIA: John, hush! Why not believe in him, my dear? I believe in him, and I am not afraid to say so. Nor, with all my long years of sad experience, am I a corruptionist.

MRS. LEE: Then do you think democracy the best government? Is it really and truly successful, after all?

LYDIA: How direct you are! You are more brutal than the Senator. These matters I seldom talk about in polite society. They are excruciating. It is like asking crumbling old ruins, with one foot in the grave, if they really and truly believe in God; what do they honestly think about a life after death, and is the universe, in their opinion, good or bad. These subjects one naturally reserves for solemn reflection, in private decay. But since you have asked this ancient party for her political creed, well, you shall have it. American Democracy insists that the great masses are now raised to a higher level than ever before, and will be raised higher. That is its central movement. And if it carries on its surface waves of scum and filth, underneath, where the currents flow, the waters are clear. Everything will be carried forward. Broken, perhaps, but forward. I grant you it is only an experiment, but it satisfies society's deepest instinct: to struggle within itself. Badly, in blood and rage, like a terrible family, but every other possible step is passive, looks backward toward fathers and kings, and unchangeable domination. Why do that? Why not force society to struggle with issues vital to its daily existence; issues only a fool or a suicide can ignore.

MRS. LEE: But suppose your experiment fails? Suppose human beings are too corrupt? Suppose the struggle you say lies at the heart of democracy becomes so strong it tears us all apart? Suppose democracy destroys itself?

LYDIA: Ah, well, then, my dear Mrs. Lee, I should spend my days at the Washington Observatory. Come with me there, sometime. Have you ever made the acquaintance of a fixed star? They say that there are twenty millions of them now, just in sight, and each a sun, just like ours. Just as big. Just as hot. Just as beautiful. Just as crucial to some other form of life. And when one of those twenty millions of fixed stars suddenly glows in the night, with a quick bright sparkle, what has happened, do you think? Why, a satellite, like our own little planet here, like our little nation that we love, and its government that we cherish and have created with our blood, but which, for all that, is only a government like any other, has fallen, has plunged into one of those twenty million suns, and is burning up. Its career finished, its capacities quite exhausted. Curious, isn't it, like the moth going into the candle flame? Flutter, flutter; fly to the fire. Poof.

MRS. LEE: You give me the shudders. You can believe in a country, and yet wander with cold-eyed pleasure into barren infinity. I could never follow you there.

LYDIA: Yes you could. And I have my own faith, after all. If not in the old dogmas of churches and kings, in the new ones of Science and Human Nature, both no doubt equally pompous and equally silly as the old, and equally doomed, who can tell? But let us be true to our time. Faithful to our Darwin, who will be as old as Aquinas some day, to our new Democracy, which will also age, like the Divine Right of Kings, and perhaps fall, taking us with it. If our age is to be beaten, let us die in the ranks where we belong. If it is to be victorious, then let us be the first to lead the columns.

146

But let us not, for goodness' sakes, sulk, grumble and pout! There! Now get me out of here, Jacobi, before I ruin my reputation as a cynic. Ladies and gentlemen, good night.

[*She goes out with* JACOBI. MRS. LEE *and everyone else follows, to see her to the door and say good-by. The room is empty, much good-bying coming from the front of the house. Everyone else is leaving, too.* RAITCLIFFE *walks into the room, quietly, alone.* MRS. LEE *returns.*]

MRS. LEE: Oh.

RAITCLIFFE: I waited to say good-by.

MRS. LEE: I'm so glad you did. I hope you're not angry with Baron Jacobi. I'm certain he did not mean to be rude.

RAITCLIFFE: Your innocence is an April breeze. Baron Jacobi is kept here by his country because of his scandals, debts and temper. He is a pederast, who suffers unspeakable diseases. Vipers, Mrs. Lee, not flowers, suit him best. We have never amused each other, the Baron and I, and he has scarched and searched for a quarrel between us.

MRS. LEE: My sweet little Baron Jacobi? Are you joking?

RAITCLIFFE: If we were in Bulgaria now, your sweet little Baron Jacobi would find a way to insult me, and on some pretty dueling field at dawn, put a bullet in my head. He's famous for that, at home.

MRS. LEE: Oh, dear.

RAITCLIFFE: Your first lesson in politics, a difficult game for ladies. It is all a matter of life or death.

MRS. LEE: I see. Thank you so much.

RAITCLIFFE: Welcome. But I didn't come to teach. I came to learn. [*He picks up a book from her table.*] *The Origin of Species. Well.* [*He opens it.*] Autographed, I see. Very impressive.

MRS. LEE: Thank you.

[*There is a moment's pause.*]

RAITCLIFFE: Well, don't you have some Walter Scott somewhere? I know what to say about Walter Scott.

MRS. LEE [*grinning now*]: No, Senator. It's Darwin, or nothing. You said you came to learn.

RAITCLIFFE: All right. Do you understand this book?

MRS. LEE: Not very well. I am only a poor female.

RAITCLIFFE: Do you want to understand it? Why? Why —ah—what *public good*, for instance, will it do?

MRS. LEE [*thinking*]: It might teach us modesty, if nothing else.

RAITCLIFFE: Because it says we are descended from monkeys?

MRS. LEE: Exactly.

RAITCLIFFE: Do you think we are descended from monkeys?

MRS. LEE: Why not?

RAITCLIFFE: Speaking for myself, I don't like the connection. Mrs. Lee, this book degrades our divine nature, reducing man to the level of brutes. That Jacobi or Carrington would embrace such doctrines, I can understand, but that you should join them is unworthy of you.

MRS. LEE: You are really very hard on the monkeys. The monkeys never did you any harm. They are not in public life. They don't even vote. But if they did, Silas Raitcliffe, I would find you bursting with enthusiasm, praising their intelligence and virtue, and calling them gods instead of gorillas. You might stop to be thankful, Senator, that this melancholy world has inherited the gaiety of the monkeys, as well as their chatter and their public speech!

RAITCLIFFE: I am routed, completely. I will very humbly go home.

MRS. LEE: Oh, please, sit down. I don't mean to hurt your feelings. I just wanted to give a nice party.

RAITCLIFFE: You also meant to secure your position in Washington society, and everyone came to watch you do it. Make no mistake about power, Mrs. Lee. Yours as a hostess, mine as a senator, Grant's as the President. It doesn't have anything to do with virtue; it isn't an intellectual puzzle. It's a wrestling match, and it demands a lot of strength. I am as experienced with it as anyone else, but I can be destroyed tomorrow. And I need your help.

MRS. LEE: What for? I don't understand.

RAITCLIFFE: Well, the President is going to ask me into the Cabinet.

MRS. LEE: Congratulations!

RAITCLIFFE: Not quite yet, I'm afraid. The President means to get me out of the Senate, into the Cabinet, and then, out of the Cabinet, into the street.

MRS. LEE: Would he do that?

RAITCLIFFE: Do you know how many Cabinet changes he has made during his administration?

MRS. LEE: No.

RAITCLIFFE: Twenty-five.

MRS. LEE: Oh.

RAITCLIFFE: If I go in, I am lost. If I refuse, I have provoked a quarrel with the President, disgraced the party, and will be as welcome for future nominations as a boa constrictor. What shall I do?

MRS. LEE: I beg your pardon?

RAITCLIFFE: That is what I stayed to ask you. What shall I do?

[MRS. LEE *looks at him, seriously and quite earnestly. She thinks a moment, then answers openly and firmly.*]

MRS. LEE: Whatever is best for the *public good!*

RAITCLIFFE: Pardon me?

MRS. LEE: Whatever is best for the *public good!*

[*He stares at her, shakes his head, smiling, and looks at her again.*]

RAITCLIFFE: But what *is* best for the public good! That is the dilemma none of you really face. You run away and talk reform. Do you know what Carrington said to me while you were out of the room?

MRS. LEE: Please, let's not fight about our friends.

RAITCLIFFE: Yours, not mine. Come, come, you ask me for honesty. Won't *you* admit they all detest me, and mean to turn you against me, if they can? Admit that, now, Madeleine. Is it the truth, yes or no?

MRS. LEE: Yes.

RAITCLIFFE: Of course it is. Once, when you were out of the room, your friend Carrington insinuated I could practice reform when I had to. Everyone knew what he meant. In the worst years of the war, my state was certain to be carried by a peace party. There was not the slightest doubt in my mind that the public good, the fate of the nation, depended on that election. I was then Governor of Illinois. Upon me the responsibility rested. I controlled the northern counties, telegraphed their officials on Election Day to overbalance our losses, and give the state to us. They did. I am not proud of the transaction but I would do it again, painful as it was, *for the public good.* But, of course, I cannot expect your Mr. Carrington to approve such unseemly action. For he, then, was carrying out his principles of reform by rebellion and treason in the armies of the Confederacy!

MRS. LEE: Oh.

RAITCLIFFE: But do not spare me. Tell me I am only a coarse and greedy politician who doesn't care who makes the people's wars, so long as I make up their ballots.

MRS. LEE: No, please—

RAITCLIFFE: Let me have the full force of all your culti-

vated and educated irony. Tell me the man who murders the ballot box for his country is even a great
patriot, not an assassin, for he gets his seat in the
Senate as his share of the plunder. Can't you stick that
knife into me, Madeleine? A hundred men do, every
day I walk into that Senate, where you imagine I play
at making speeches.

MRS. LEE: Please. Stop.

RAITCLIFFE: Not before you give me your answer. Do I
say yes to Grant, or not? What is best for the public
good?

MRS. LEE: That you must find yourself. You will know
what it is better than I. All I can tell you is not to be
ruled by your feelings, because of me or anyone else.
You are too important a man for that, to all of us. Now,
that's enough, Senator. Let a poor provincial Manhattan
hostess repair to her closet and powder her shiny nose.

RAITCLIFFE: I thank you, then, for this wonderful afternoon. I will not forget it.

MRS. LEE: Nor will I.

RAITCLIFFE: And I didn't simply ignore what was said,
about corruption. I didn't.

MRS. LEE: Please, not all over again.

RAITCLIFFE: Yes, but you still think I am a man made out
of a Middle Western stone! That I just close my eyes
to ugliness and evil and don't give a damn what happens! Oh, I could tell you—but I will, if you let me!
Don't forget me, please! I'll see myself out! Good night!

[*And he is gone, leaving* MRS. LEE *stunned, staring*

152

after him, with a puzzled and shocked expression. The lights go down upon her as she moves away, then up again in her tracks but upon another woman, upon ESTHER, *who has replaced her, and who stands gazing in that same puzzled way, but up into the great expanse and vaulted ceilings of the Washington Cathedral. We hear slow, rich chords of ancient hymns.* ESTHER, *musing upon her life and upon the death of her father, stands in eternal space, in a radiance of stained-glass windows and soaring ceilings. Above her is the Saint Cecelia, painted upon the wall, at whom she stares.* HAZARD *appears behind her.*]

HAZARD: Welcome back.

ESTHER: Hello.

HAZARD: It's good to see you again. We've been expecting you.

ESTHER: Have you?

HAZARD: Yes, indeed.

ESTHER: I'm sorry.

HAZARD: Esther—

ESTHER: I don't know what to do. For weeks I didn't sleep. A voice, a bar of music, the smell of cigar smoke, anything makes me cry. I can't find my life again. I can't do anything. What's happened to me?

HAZARD: You're grieving. It's natural.

ESTHER: But not this much! I knew it would be terrible, but not this desolation, this torture. What's happened to me?

153

HAZARD: You've been struck by lightning. The torture is seeing what it illuminates. By the light of your father's deathbed, Esther, you've seen life as it is. No one can bear that for long. Human beings are not made for it. They can't do it. Don't try. Work! Live!

ESTHER: Oh, God, I can't.

HAZARD: Esther! Life commands us, and we must obey! To live at all can seem mockery of our deepest hopes and ideals. Even a betrayal, at times, of those we have truly loved. But life is the will of God, however terrible, and it is the meaning of this cathedral. Now, take pictures of *that!* Begin! I beg you.

ESTHER: Oh, Reverend Hazard, you do have your effect. You do give Esther Dudley some hope. I confess it. Could you take me for a walk? Just a walk in Rock Creek Park? To see the birds and the fish?

HAZARD: Give me your hand.

[*She does, and they walk away together. A Union Army war song.* PRESIDENT GRANT *strolls into his White House office. He smokes a cigar, a vile black Havana he is never without, which sends up great puffs of dingy smoke.* RAITCLIFFE *appears.*]

GRANT: Mr. Raitcliffe.

RAITCLIFFE: Mr. President.

GRANT: I sent for you to consult with you about my Cabinet replacements. Here is a list of the three gentlemen I intend to invite into it.

[*He hands a list to* RAITCLIFFE, *who takes it but does not look at it.*]

RAITCLIFFE: Thank you very much, Mr. President.

GRANT: You will see that I have got you down for the Treasury. Will you look at the rest and say what you think?

[RAITCLIFFE *calmly folds the list in two, without looking.*]

RAITCLIFFE: I have no objection to any Cabinet members you appoint, provided only that I am not among them.

GRANT: What's that?

RAITCLIFFE: My wish is to remain where I am. There I can serve your administration better than I could in the Cabinet.

GRANT: Then you refuse?

RAITCLIFFE: By no means, Mr. President. I only decline to offer any advice, or even to read the names of my proposed colleagues until it is decided that my services are absolutely necessary. If they are, and I am appointed, I shall of course accept, without caring whom I serve.

GRANT: I see. Now, Senator, your refusal is going to knock everything on the head. I thought the matter was all fixed. What more can I do?

RAITCLIFFE: Appoint me, by all means, if you so desire.

GRANT: I'm not going to yank you off that committee, and you know it. I can't. You know what I went through with Charles Sumner.

RAITCLIFFE: Yes, sir, I do. And I always thought that was a regrettable misunderstanding. I don't say I supported all your wishes in that conflict, but I did feel that Sumner was overbearing and snobbish, when he had little reason to be so.

GRANT: Did you? So did I.

RAITCLIFFE: His worship of Eastern nobility was a disgrace.

GRANT: That's what I thought.

RAITCLIFFE: That is why I want to stay where I am. In Sumner's old position. I can do my best for you, and for the party, there.

GRANT: Now, Raitcliffe, I want you to know I appreciate that, and so does the party. But you're one of the few who understand about me and Sumner. I can't let you refuse.

RAITCLIFFE: Mr. President, I am a faithful administration man. I serve my party and my country. If you can give me a day or two to mull this over, I will give you my answer.

GRANT: Done.

RAITCLIFFE: I am much obliged to your understanding.

GRANT: Don't mention it. And by the way—

RAITCLIFFE: Yes, sir?

GRANT: I'm glad to know a man of social distinction from my neck of the woods. Peoria, isn't it?

RAITCLIFFE: Yes, Mr. President.

GRANT: Right. I'm from Galena.

RAITCLIFFE: Yes, sir, I know. But what is my new social distinction?

GRANT: Why, Mrs. Lightfoot Lee.

RAITCLIFFE: I do have the honor of her acquaintance, yes, sir.

GRANT: Julia tells me she's a bright light, and Julia knows.

RAITCLIFFE: Good evening, Mr. President. It has been a great pleasure.

GRANT: Good night, Raitcliffe. Tell Mrs. Lee, Julia and I send our respects to you both.

[RAITCLIFFE *bows and leaves.* GRANT *looks after him and puffs.*]

Humph.

[*Fife and drums. Over the roll and beat of crisp Army drums, a pellucid little fife plays "Rally Round the Flag."* GRANT *listens a moment, remembering the Battle of the Wilderness, where he made the song famous, then goes, smoking, into darkness. With returning light, we see greensward, a few small trees, bushes, white iron garden chairs and benches. It is a fine summer day on the lawn at Mount Vernon. A corps of young fifers and drummers, kept up by the Mount Vernon Ladies Association of the Union, are practicing on the grounds, parading about playing marching tunes of the Continental and Union armies. Once established, the drums and the fife fade away, to be heard moving about in the distance, and onto the lawn comes* MRS. LEE, *followed by* LYDIA DUDLEY.]

MRS. LEE: Marvelous. Lydia, you were right. It's captivating.

LYDIA: When the weather is good, yes, it is.

MRS. LEE: That quaint garden, and this ragged lawn. The great river in front, and the old fort. The haze in the air. It softens everything.

LYDIA: Except those drums. The Mount Vernon Ladies Association of the Union takes its custodial duties seriously, I see.

MRS. LEE: Age, and peace. Yet only ten miles over that river, the Capitol glares in harsh sunlight, and the citizens rage.

RAITCLIFFE [*joining them*]: That Capitol at the moment, let me tell you, is bursting with office seekers. If mine had guessed where I was going, they would have swamped the boat. Illinois alone would have shown us all a watery grave.

[*They move down, to look out over the river.* ESTHER, *with her camera,* STRONG *and* HAZARD *come on together,* ESTHER *rather consciously avoiding* HAZARD *and clinging to* STRONG, *who carries a book about Mount Vernon.*]

ESTHER: Well, of course it's old, Stephen. It's a plantation. Tell us about it, George.

HAZARD: Oh, dear. The crunch of geology. Listen, George, I left my prayer book in Washington; you leave your pick and shovel. Let's be sensible and have something to drink. Where's the champagne?

[CARRINGTON *enters, carrying buckets of champagne bottles in crushed ice. He wears a large floppy darkgrey wool hat and a very long dark-grey cloak. With him is* JACOBI, *in his hands a tray of champagne glasses.* CARRINGTON *dumps the buckets and pops the first cork, as the marching fife and drum music comes closer. They all enjoy their champagne. When the drums have faded,* HAZARD *moves to* LYDIA.]

HAZARD: Miss Dudley, I've heard your father was very intimate with George Washington. Will you forgive me if I ask, did you ever know him?

LYDIA: My father, young man, or George Washington?

HAZARD: George Washington.

LYDIA: You have the gall to ask me that?

HAZARD: I do.

LYDIA: You pursue a dignified lady into the sanctity of her great age and demand your favors, you nasty priest?

HAZARD: I do.

LYDIA: Wonderful. Yes, I knew him. General Washington died when I was a child, but I remember him very well. What do *you* think he was like, Reverend Hazard? What is your conception of the father of your country?

HAZARD: I see a stern face, like Stuart's portrait. I see Olympian detachment, a firm mouth but soft and searching eyes, and that handsome large brow and head. I see a man who could have seized all the powers of a dictator, when they were his for the asking, but who refused them. I would give anything to have known him, and to have served him.

LYDIA: Would you, really? Well, the truth is, you charming young priest, General Washington was a rawboned country farmer. He was very hard-featured, very awkward, and very dull. He was very bad-tempered, very profane, and generally tipsy after dinner. He also pinched his wife a great deal, and made her cry.

[*They are all pleasantly scandalized. In the distance, the fife and drum corps is playing "Yankee Doodle."*]

MRS. LEE: Lydia! That's shocking!

LYDIA: Oh, no, it isn't. We're all patriotic about Washington, and like to hide his faults. You've heard Parson Weems's stirring parable of the cherry tree, the hatchet, and the truth? Well, I cannot tell a lie, *either*, and the truth is even as a small boy George Washington had a temper so violent nothing could be done with him. One day in a fit he cut down all his father's fruit trees. And when he was accused, he not only admitted doing it, he tried to scalp the farm hands and brain his own father with that little hatchet, which was, of course, a four-hand broadaxe. That's how *that* got started!

MRS. LEE [*to* CARRINGTON]: John, defend General Washington. He's a fellow Virginian. Save his reputation.

[CARRINGTON *smiles. He takes off his wool hat, and pins two tips of the brim up against the crown, making a three-cornered eighteenth-century hat.*]

CARRINGTON: He had a temper, all right. He chased a man out of the house once, for stammering. He couldn't tolerate anybody who stammered. He was a miser, too. He made a claim against the estate of a house painter for fifteen shillings. He took it to court. And won.

[*He sets the hat down, picks up a large stick and pins another to it, making a rough cross. He finds some branches, with twiggy fingers at their ends, and takes the leaves off them.*]

RAITCLIFFE: Signs of a man obsessed with trifles, fussing over small details.

JACOBI: Such as the foundation of the Republic? This conversation verges on treason. I have never heard anything so delightful in all my life.

LYDIA [*to* HAZARD]: Well, young man? What do you say now?

HAZARD: I say what difference does it make? Suppose he did apply his principles to bill collecting, or nightcaps or feather dusters or anything else? At least he had some principles to apply! I still stand in awe of him.

LYDIA: Good for you. Stand your ground. You're wrong, but stand your ground.

[CARRINGTON *has now uprooted a small bush. He has rammed the large stick down through the lacework of the iron bench. It has a crosspiece and two dangling sticks. The bush is also impaled by the large stick. He finds a gourd, which he sticks on the top of the stick.*]

CARRINGTON: In my family, he was simply a homesick Virginia planter. Europe gave him that enormous reputation for not making himself king of America, but he never had the chance, really. He'd have looked like a fool, and he knew it. He'd have been deposed with laughter. The truth is, he was a farmer; all he wanted was this: Mount Vernon.

[CARRINGTON *has now created a man's body, with a stick for a spine, crosspiece for shoulders, branches for arms and fingers, a shrub for a torso, and a faceless gourd for a head. He will swing his large cloak over it*

161

all, and place his now three-cornered hat on the gourd, making a quite striking figure, sitting on the ironwork bench. "Yankee Doodle" gets louder.]

LYDIA: But for all this, we idolize him; cynical old ladies and drunken artists won't change that. Therefore, the only decent thing to do is be gracious, and offer him a toast, with this nice champagne.

[*As she raises her glass,* CARRINGTON *puts final touches on his creation.*]

I give you the crude man I knew as a child, who blew his nose with his hand, and who has now become Morality, Justice, Duty, Truth. Eternal Righteousness in a uniform: austere, solitary, grand: a god.

[*The fife and drum corps tears into a final chorus of "Yankee Doodle" and they stand quite still, champagne in hand, stricken by the presence of a preposterous George Washington, sitting on his lawn at Mount Vernon. The music dies away. The people just stand there, looking, for a long time. Many people have many thoughts. It is* MRS. LEE, *finally, who breaks the silence.*]

MRS. LEE: *But at least he was honest!*

LYDIA: Yes, he was.

CARRINGTON: Which is why he was such a clumsy politician? What do you think, Senator Raitcliffe?

MRS. LEE: Now, John.

RAITCLIFFE: That's all right. Washington wasn't a politician at all, Carrington, as we understand the word.

CARRINGTON: How do we understand the word?

RAITCLIFFE: Differently. He stood outside politics. That can't be done today.

MRS. LEE: Why not? Why couldn't you do it today?

RAITCLIFFE: I couldn't because I'd be laughed out of town. Like George Washington there, trying to be king.

CARRINGTON: But Washington *didn't* try to be king. Untangling your thoughts, Senator, is an infernal nuisance. What you mean is, Washington was too respectable for times like ours. Yes?

RAITCLIFFE: No, I mean this: if George Washington were President now, he'd either learn our ways or lose his next election. In a hurry. Only fools and children cry for the moon and the stars. Especially when there's another man right behind you, trying to put you out of office. As true in Washington's day as it is now, and it always will be!

JACOBI: Delicious corruption! Treason in the open air. I feel like dancing.

ESTHER: Well, I feel like taking a walk. That champagne and all these speeches and the father of my country there have all gone to my head. [*Takes her camera*] Lydia, will you come with me while I do the house?

LYDIA: With pleasure, my pet.

HAZARD: May I join you?

ESTHER: Oh, yes, of course. George, you, too. Anyone else?

[*They all get up, except* MRS. LEE *and* RAITCLIFFE, *and begin to move off toward the mansion house.* CAR-

163

RINGTON *lingers, unwilling to leave* MRS. LEE *and* RAITCLIFFE *alone.*]

MRS. LEE: Aren't you going, too, John? You promised me a sketch of the house, remember?

CARRINGTON: Of course.

[*He adjusts George Washington's hat a bit, and leaves him as chaperon for them.* MRS. LEE *and* RAITCLIFFE *face each other, with the seated figure of General Washington between them.*]

RAITCLIFFE: I'm going to hold you to your promise.

MRS. LEE: What has happened?

RAITCLIFFE: President Grant has me on the hip, that's what's happened. I have until tomorrow to decide.

MRS. LEE: What are you going to do?

RAITCLIFFE: That is what I am asking you. What shall I do?

MRS. LEE: Oh, my.

RAITCLIFFE: Everything finally comes to a decision, you see. Well?

MRS. LEE: Please. Don't.

RAITCLIFFE: But I must! I'm up against the wall, my dear Mrs. Lee. You have shown some interest in me, I believe? Can you sit twirling a fan while my enemies bring about my destruction? They mean to ruin me, and end my public life. Do you understand that?

MRS. LEE: I do. I do.

RAITCLIFFE: I honestly want to do my duty. But what is

164

it? You told me I should not be ruled by my feelings. That personal consideration should have no weight. Did you not?

MRS. LEE: Yes, I think so. I think I did.

RAITCLIFFE: Very well. I throw them all away. My Washington career, my reputation of twenty-five years in the Congress, I toss them into the Potomac there, over the body of George Washington. Gone. Now tell me what to do.

MRS. LEE: Please, Silas.

RAITCLIFFE: I see it in your face. You think I must go into the Cabinet, accept my duty, and disregard the consequences.

MRS. LEE: I don't know. Yes. I think that would be my feeling. Yes, I think so.

RAITCLIFFE: And when I fall a sacrifice to Ulysses Grant's envy and intrigue, what will you say then, my dear lady? Like everyone else, that I was a fool! You don't gain the trust of a nation by making a sacrifice of yourself; you do it by winning what you want. I don't want to be a sacrifice; I do want a nomination! I parade no high moral views. I won't cant about virtue. But I claim a worthy public life, during which I have done my very best every single living moment! Do you believe that?

MRS. LEE: Yes, I do. And if you yourself know it, if you are certain you have done what is right, isn't that finally the only real reward a decent man ever has?

RAITCLIFFE: Oh, you are a hard critic! You are the judge

165

who never practiced law. You condemn by abstract principles and bolts of divine justice. But when I come to you, as I do now, on the verge of what is likely to be the fatal plunge of my life, and ask you for some clue to the moral principle to guide me, you look on, refuse to soil your gloves, and tell me, while I stand choking to death, that virtue is its own reward! And you don't even tell me where that virtue is!

MRS. LEE: I confess my sins. Life is more complicated than I thought.

RAITCLIFFE: Very well. I'm going to do it, for you. I will walk into that den of lions, since you obviously think I should. But I will also hold you to *your* responsibility. You can't refuse, now, to stand by me, and see me through all the dangers you have brought upon me.

MRS. LEE: No, no! No responsibilities, I beg you. You ask more than I can give.

RAITCLIFFE: But duty is duty, for you as well as for me! I have a right to the help of an honest mind and you have no right to refuse me! How *can* you reject your own responsibilities, and still hold *me* to *mine!*

[*He leaves her, quickly.* MRS. LEE *sits stunned by the passion, drive and force of the man. In the distance, the drums and the fife are playing through the "Camp Duties of the Continental Army," which give to the fife stately melodies.* MRS. LEE *stands listening, gazing at the seated figure, who seems to listen with her.* ESTHER *comes strolling down from the mansion house, alone. They stand together on the lawn of Mount Vernon, two very lovely American women.*]

166

MRS. LEE: How was the house?

ESTHER: Quiet, and comforting. Everything there is peaceful, even down to George Washington's little bedroom. I wanted to lie down in it, and sleep away a century or two.

MRS. LEE: How lovely that would be. Well, I suppose I should join the others. Are you all right here alone?

ESTHER: Yes.

[MRS. LEE *turns, faces the house, then stops. The fife plays in the distance.*]

MRS. LEE: Must I feel so sad, looking at that house? Why is it that everything Washington touched, he purified, while everything we touch, we soil? And in spite of the Senator, Esther, isn't it perhaps better to *be* a child, and cry for the moon and the stars?

ESTHER: I don't know.

MRS. LEE: Nor I.

[*She goes.* ESTHER *listens to the fife and the drums. Then she hears someone coming. It is* HAZARD.]

HAZARD [*passionately*]: I can't follow you about any more. I love you, Esther, with all my heart! You must love me! You will. Marry me! I will adore you and protect you for the rest of your life!

ESTHER: Oh, you fool! You blockhead! Of course I love you! Of course I will marry you!

[*And she runs off.* HAZARD *stands blinking for a moment, then runs after her.*]

HAZARD: Esther! Esther!

[*The lawn is now deserted, except for its owner, the figure of George Washington, who sits as if listening to the fife and the drum. Laughter comes down from the mansion house, and over it, over his estate, the seated figure seems to brood. On the long, steady drum roll that ends all Revolutionary marching tunes, the stage is brought to darkness, but not before it seems, in the dying light, that there has been a dip of ancestral shoulders and a twitch of an ancient hand.*]

Act Two: The Future

[*Hymns. Light on the upturned face of* ESTHER DUD-
LEY. *The voice of* STEPHEN HAZARD *is heard preach-
ing.*]

VOICE OF HAZARD: —for struggle as you will, you cannot
escape. You must live by faith. Do not doubt, believe!
Believe in your life, and it will prosper! In your cause,
and it will grow! In your country, and it will triumph!
Belief is nothing less than Love itself, the great magnet
of the world, which holds creation together.

ESTHER: I don't believe it!

[*The light fades from her troubled face, but in a moment it comes back on, illuminating now another
woman in her place:* MRS. LEE. *It is as if one woman has
merged into the other. The light now spreads brightly
over the rest of the stage. Around* MRS. LEE *the stage
has been arranged into one huge Washington parlor in
the abstract, which belongs to any and all of them. At
the rear, there are two drape-and-pillar openings, for
entrance and exit.* MRS. LEE *now stands musing, waiting for a caller. She holds a small oil painting in a gilt
frame, looks at it with wry but real attachment, sets
it on a small table, and turns to meet her visitor.*]

MRS. LEE: Mrs. Baker. I am so glad to see you.

MRS. BAKER: My dear Mrs. Lee, what a pleasure! I hope

you don't mind my dropping down on you right out of the bright-blue sky!

MRS. LEE: Not at all.

MRS. BAKER: Oh, look at that! What a sweet little picture. Japanese, isn't it? Seaweed seen right through a fog?

MRS. LEE: Not exactly. It is a Corot. I got it in Europe last winter.

MRS. BAKER: Did you really? I went to an auction yesterday, and do you know I bought a teapot with a picture painted on it just like that. It was Japanese, though.

MRS. LEE: What a coincidence.

MRS. BAKER: Yes, isn't it? Well, since Mr. Baker's death, I don't do so much now. Got more time to shop.

MRS. LEE: You have certainly had an interesting life in Washington. I envy you the skills you learned in your lobby. You must be a very able diplomat.

MRS. BAKER: Oh, I worked lots harder than diplomats. We knew half of Congress intimately, all of them by sight. Where they came from and what they liked. I could get around the great part of them, sooner or later.

MRS. LEE: Do you mean you managed to have all those Congressmen vote as you pleased?

MRS. BAKER: Well! We got our bills through!

MRS. LEE: But how? Did they take bribes?

MRS. BAKER: Some of them did. Some liked suppers and theatre and cards and all sorts of pretty things. Some had to be led, and some banged on the snout like Paddy's pig, but all of them were flattered, you know.

MRS. LEE: But if there was difficulty, did you and your husband actually bring pressure to bear on a Congressman yourself?

MRS. BAKER: Sometimes, in different ways. Some had wives we could handle, and then, best of all, some *didn't* have wives, if you know what I mean. That made it easy. You know what I mean?

MRS. LEE: Unfortunately, yes. But how would you have gone after a respectable Senator's vote? A man like Senator Raitcliffe, for instance?

MRS. BAKER: Oh, my dear, it wasn't all that shady. What we wanted was generally all right; just now and then, when a lot of money and a close vote were involved, well, then we did have to find out what each vote was worth. Oh, so many things I've seen. My goodness, I've already told you more than I ought. I already think of you as an old friend.

MRS. LEE: That's very kind of you.

MRS. BAKER: Not one bit. And that brings me to the reason for this visit. I wanted to come and just ask you plain out if we can congratulate you and the Senator. Nothing would give us all more pleasure.

MRS. LEE: I'm sorry to disappoint you. It is kind of you to take an interest, but this particular lobby is closed, I'm afraid.

MRS. BAKER: Oh, you. That's real funny. I think wit is just wonderful. Wish I had some myself, but I just have to pound along best I can. I certainly have enjoyed looking at this picture. It's a beauty. You certainly will have to come see me, soon, and bring this with you,

171

hear? I certainly got some friends would just love to see it.

[*She goes out.* MRS. LEE *stares after her with distrust and exits. Enter* LYDIA *and* JACOBI.]

LYDIA: Yesterday when Stephen brought over the ring, he found Esther on the sofa surrounded by all her father's books on religion. The Chief Justice, you know, was something less than pious. Stephen took one look at what Esther was reading and his hair stood on end. I'm afraid it's a crisis. This morning, when I took Esther for a drive, she was in tears over the Atonement, and this afternoon I believe she has gone to bed with a headache over the Athansian Creed.

JACOBI: Hazard is a good fellow at heart. What does it matter?

LYDIA: He is indeed a fine fellow, but at heart he is an American priest, and it matters a great deal. He packs that church every Sunday. People come from all over the country now to hear him. Esther is the only one who doesn't want to listen.

JACOBI: Is she jealous?

LYDIA: Partly. She doesn't want to share her man with a congregation, as she must, but that's every church wife's little cross. No, she has to believe what her husband says in that church is the truth, and she knows she doesn't.

JACOBI: She'll give in.

LYDIA: She can't. She has to make a conscious choice. Otherwise, she will be an unhappily married woman for life, or Reverend Hazard must leave his church. Either way there will be a divorce. There is really very nasty gossip about her in that church already, and I don't like the sound of it.

[*Enter* CARRINGTON]

John, there you are. We've been waiting for you.

CARRINGTON: Sorry. Hello, Jacobi, honey.

JACOBI: *Mon ami.*

LYDIA: John, I want to tell you about a call that will be paid on you sometime tomorrow. Do be as sober as possible; it's the D.A.R.

CARRINGTON: The D.A.R.?

LYDIA: I proposed the encounter. I am telling you about it now so we shall be spared drunken surprise and obscene salutations. Do be ready to receive us properly.

CARRINGTON: What for?

LYDIA: You will be formally asked to give a lecture to the D.A.R. On some subject that appeals to you, remotely connected perhaps with American art. I hope you will do it. I was told to come up with something startling.

CARRINGTON: I am overwhelmed.

LYDIA: No, you're not. God knows what you'll say. But they asked for it. Now then, have we got the blankets and the chicken and the wine?

JACOBI: All in the carriage.

LYDIA: Good. John, what are you up to? Do you see Madeleine Lee this evening?

CARRINGTON: I fear not. The Senator exercises his prerogative.

LYDIA: Well, come along to the Observatory and picnic with us. Bring your bourbon and your aching heart, and when night falls we'll look at the stars. Can you come?

CARRINGTON: Well—

LYDIA: It will do you good. We're ancient crockery, all of us, but we spread our blankets on the lawn, feast and chat, and after dusk, watch the stars. And, John, if on this outing there is brash and rather vulgar band music, as there sometimes is, it really sounds much softer and nicer there, under the great stars. Cheer up.

[*They exit. Enter* GRANT *and* RAITCLIFFE.]

GRANT: That's another one. I refer it to you.

RAITCLIFFE: Fine. I don't think there will be any repercussion.

GRANT: You just said *no?*

RAITCLIFFE: A blunt refusal was safe. They left.

GRANT: I have been trying to get rid of them for a month. How'd you do it?

RAITCLIFFE: Allow me my secrets. Tomorrow might require a considerable pledge.

GRANT: Just get rid of them. What else?

RAITCLIFFE: The speech. Here it is. I made these few trifling notes, hoping they might be of some small value as you do the final draft.

GRANT: Thanks, Raitcliffe.

RAITCLIFFE: You can just copy it out from this. Now, I did have some trouble with all the people on that list.

GRANT: What's the matter? No more jobs?

RAITCLIFFE: There weren't *any*. It will be necessary to effect a few—ah—removals here and there, to provide for them.

GRANT: Raitcliffe, I leave that to you. You'll do it right; I know that.

RAITCLIFFE: Thank you, sir.

GRANT: Not at all. I'm not afraid to say I was wrong. I was wrong about you, Raitcliffe, and I admit that right now.

RAITCLIFFE: Mr. President—

GRANT: No, no. There it is. I said it, and that means it is said. Now, Raitcliffe, you know my plans of supporting the Vice President are all knocked on the head.

RAITCLIFFE: Well, yes. Why did he let himself get caught?

GRANT: I don't know, but he did. And the field, so far as I'm concerned, is open. A nomination is not far away. I want you to know, Raitcliffe, that I recognize your position in the party. I won't stand in your way.

RAITCLIFFE: I am deeply affected, Mr. President.

GRANT: And maybe I can do more than that. Well, here's Julia.

[JULIA GRANT *comes in, pleasant, open, spirited, cross-eyed.*]

175

RAITCLIFFE: Mrs. Grant.

JULIA: Secretary Raitcliffe. How's Mrs. Lee?

RAITCLIFFE: I beg your pardon?

GRANT: Now, Raitcliffe, as long as we are talking we might as well talk. You got this one weakness. Your wife died all those years ago. You've been a free man too long, Raitcliffe.

RAITCLIFFE: I lack your good fortune, Mr. President. The gods do not smile on everyone, as they smile on you.

JULIA: They didn't always smile, Secretary. The President and I had our hard times, before the war. Didn't we, President?

GRANT: Julia, it's true.

JULIA: I don't know what we'd have done, in those days, without each other. And I for one, Secretary, don't want to see any man in high office around here without a good faithful woman to help him out. Isn't that right, President?

GRANT: Julia, it is. Think about it, Raitcliffe.

RAITCLIFFE: I promise to do so, Mr. President.

GRANT: Good.

JULIA: Come along with me a minute then, Secretary. I just want to know more about Mrs. Lightfoot Lee. I like her a lot.

[*She takes him off.* GRANT *watches them go, puffs on his cigar.*]

GRANT: Heh, heh.

[*He goes off, in a swirl of black Havana smoke. Enter* MRS. LEE *followed by* CARRINGTON]

MRS. LEE: John, I'm not going to talk about it.

CARRINGTON: My dear Madeleine, you think you have all these choices. You don't. They ran out long ago.

MRS. LEE: Ridiculous. With your whiskey glass in your hand, you lecture me on the evils of dishonorable men. I'm very tired of it.

CARRINGTON: He is a dishonorable man. If he'd hauled you off to his boardinghouse bed, and made you like it better than your own, or mine, I wouldn't say a word. But you really have been seduced, madam, corrupted by his obscene trust in your own greed. If you refuse him, he will paint your reputation black as coal. Don't you think he can claim, legitimately, that you were nothing but a cold coquette? A trifler with a decent man's affections? A tramp who turned a Senator's head?

MRS. LEE: How dare you say that! He isn't anything like that! You're terribly unfair to him.

CARRINGTON: And to you! For you love Silas Raitcliffe, no doubt, for the tenderness of his sensibilities and the shape of his head. You're full of lust, too, now, you see?

MRS. LEE [*sadly*]: And I think the world of you. How ugly life is.

CARRINGTON: And how unfair. Are you going to marry him?

MRS. LEE: You have absolutely no right to ask me that!

CARRINGTON: Then who does? Who else but me, while

you spent your days chasing that blockhead through the streets of Washington, kept you warm at night?

MRS. LEE: I would love you if I could. I can't.

CARRINGTON: Of course not. You can only get into bed with me. It is Silas Raitcliffe whose thrilling knight-errantry makes your aging heart pound. Very well. But you will pay me this much for my gallantry. Has he asked you to marry him?

MRS. LEE: He has.

CARRINGTON: Are you going to do it?

MRS. LEE: Yes, I think I am. Will you make me tell you why?

CARRINGTON: To belong to something. Something that matters.

MRS. LEE: And is that so dishonest of me?

CARRINGTON: Not at all! But it is why you will perish, later. Which is why I am going to stop you. I'm not going to let you marry that pompous lizard.

MRS. LEE: Is that so? You say you are going to stop me?

CARRINGTON: I do.

MRS. LEE: May I ask how?

CARRINGTON: In the grand tradition: here!

[*With dramatic self-mockery, but with real purpose, as well, he holds out a letter.* MRS. LEE *looks at it and him, and speaks with slow disgust.*]

MRS. LEE: What—is—that?

CARRINGTON: A letter, my lady. It will explain all. If you

have the courage to read it. It's in his own hand, Madeleine.

MRS. LEE: Disgusting.

CARRINGTON: Oh, no, it isn't. I've enjoyed being taken to bed, and I mean to reward you for it. With this letter. Do you know who gave it to me?

MRS. LEE: No, and I don't care.

CARRINGTON: Mrs. Samuel Baker. Puzzle that out. I didn't even have to go searching; it came to me. The woman likes my hands, it seems, and told me she thought they would know what to do with this letter. God knows what she has against Raitcliffe, but here it is. Take it.

MRS. LEE: No.

CARRINGTON: Then I will leave it here. [*He places it on a table, setting it up against a lamp.*] And if you are too proud to look at it, come to the cathedral a few weeks after your marriage. I will find a place for you in the Last Judgment. Read that letter and you'll know where. Good night.

[*He leaves.* MRS. LEE *stares at the letter.*]

MRS. LEE: No. It's too absurd.

[*She takes up the letter, tears it in half, starts to throw the pieces away, keeps them, and exits. Enter* JACOBI, *talking to a trapped* RAITCLIFFE, *who scowls more and more as* JACOBI *talks.*]

JACOBI: Yes, Senator, once upon a time, I also was a good party man.

RAITCLIFFE: Were you indeed, sir?

JACOBI: Yes, indeed I was, sir. My party, however, was the church. As a matter of fact, Senator, you stole your entire party system from the Roman Catholic Church. Do you know that?

RAITCLIFFE: No, I don't, sir.

JACOBI: Why, yes. Our Curia became your National Convention, and you abdicate reason, as we do, before its decisions. Our Jesuits are your delegates; our Inquisitors your political bosses. And you, Senator Raitcliffe, you are a Cardinal, sir. You should be dressed in scarlet majesty instead of that drab wool, for Cardinals are exceptional and able men. Princes, in fact. I have known quite a few; several are among my dearest friends; all are faithful to the party, but I never yet knew one who was a reformer. Now what do you say to that? What are you going to do about that?

RAITCLIFFE: How long have you been in Washington, Baron Jacobi?

JACOBI: Thirty years.

RAITCLIFFE: I see. Well, it is always a pleasure to talk to you, sir. Good day to you.

[*They exit. Enter* ESTHER *and* MRS. LEE.]

ESTHER: What do I care if he worships Zeus or Thor, for that matter. I will, too, if he does. I love him. And then he opens his mouth in that pulpit, and all those beautiful words drive me home in a rage. What is a girl to do?

MRS. LEE: Have some of my Spanish brandy. Here we are. You can use a little of this, and so can I.

ESTHER: You?

MRS. LEE [*pouring from a decanter*]: Me.

ESTHER: What on earth is troubling you?

MRS. LEE: I came to this town, you know, in cold blood. I meant to live again, whatever the price. Is that brandy good?

ESTHER: Yes, very. Go ahead, please.

MRS. LEE: No one here knows what really happened to me. How suddenly my husband died; how fond I was of him. I was very quiet about it. Then, a week later, my baby girl died of diphtheria. She suffered, and I was wild. Violent. I raved about death and God and resignation. I became stupid and dull and walked around like a machine. I traveled. I drank. And then, after four years of sorrow, it lifted. And I said, "I know what I'll do. I'll go to Washington."

ESTHER: And has Washington helped?

MRS. LEE: Well, I'm not bored any more. I'm frightened.

ESTHER: Of Senator Raitcliffe?

MRS. LEE: Of Washington.

ESTHER: This may sound silly, and I don't mean to be presumptuous, but don't you love him?

MRS. LEE: My dear, the man is likely to be nominated for the Presidency of the United States. As an antidote for a bored widow, you must admit that does have a certain pull.

ESTHER: Does he love you?

MRS. LEE: He would be good to me. There is an attraction.

181

But—do you remember, Esther, Julia Grant's reception? How long ago that seems now. How the vista has changed. I remembered it for quite a while through a sort of thrilling haze. How exciting everyone was! How potent, and dangerous, and handsome! But the mist blew away, and now—now—

ESTHER: Yes. What now?

MRS. LEE: Now there they stand. The President and his lady. As stiff and false as the front of a shop, their famous faces stripped of any signs of intelligence. Right hands stuck out toward a column of visitors, like toy dolls. I try to laugh, but it isn't funny. There they stand, automatons, chosen representatives of the strange society streaming past them. What a solemn spectacle. What a warning for an ambitious widow. How fascinating, and how deadly. They think it is all as American as a New England Sunday morning; to me it is the vision of an opium eater! My God, Esther, we will all grow up to be wax images, and our talk will be the squeaking of tiny dolls! We will wander all around the earth, and shake hands. No one will do anything else. It will be worse than Dante's *Inferno!*

ESTHER: Then why do you stay? Senator Raitcliffe?

MRS. LEE: Frankly, yes. My success in finding something to give myself up to dazzles me. I have discovered the high altar, you see. All I have to do now is crawl up there, loosen my robes a little, and bare my throat.

ESTHER: A sacrifice. I thought that was something little girls outgrew.

MRS. LEE: Not completely.

ESTHER: It's the same thing, then.

MRS. LEE: I beg your pardon?

ESTHER: I came to ask your advice. But if you must make up your mind, all alone, about Senator Raitcliffe, and the government of the United States, then the least I can do is to face Stephen Hazard and the Episcopal Church.

MRS. LEE: Well, my dear, they are both remarkable institutions, and remarkable men.

ESTHER: I know. Shall we just marry them, then?

MRS. LEE: Oh, why not?

ESTHER: May I have some more brandy?

MRS. LEE: You may have the whole bottle, Esther. Let's take it into the garden, and watch the flowers grow. They do it so easily.

[*They exit. Enter* CARRINGTON, *drunk. In his hand, a glass dark with whiskey, but in his eyes clear anguish, real pain. He smiles now across the footlights at an audience of distinguished ladies.*]

CARRINGTON: Daughters of the American Revolution! I speak to you today upon the subject of American art. I can do that. I'm an American artist, painting, in your new cathedral, a Last Judgment. I wish I could say it was a good one. It ain't. But don't worry. Nobody will care. It's big. It looks rich. And it is a technical marvel! You talk about the technique, the construction. You never mention what isn't there. What the hidden failure was. Nobody tells you. You won't know about it. But I do. And that's what I mean to talk about. [*He*

183

drinks, smiles in pain, weaves a little.] Daughters of
the Revolution, what is the trick of the Last Judgment?
It's that astonished face about to be judged, that
creature, dumbfounded, who's never been judged before. *There.* Right there, you either paint it, or you
don't. Once I went to war for my country. I believed in
it heart and soul, and one fine day I killed my brother.
Shot him in the head on a battlefield in Virginia. Went
to Paris, to drink. But I painted only models in suffering. Ravaged, maimed, dying: the final corruption of
life. I consorted with surgeons, got intimate with hospital stench. And then—what do you know, ladies—
I got myself married. To a woman dying of arsenic
poison. I saved her. She was an actress from a cheap
theatre. Medea! Clytemnestra! Glorious! I loved her.
She was more morbid than I was. We decided to die
for art. Well, we painted and drank, and it was all a
farce, but do you know, she hangs today in the Louvre.
My Omphale, Priestess, in agony on the stones of
Delphi. But Omphale became a heroine from a cheap
melodrama, screaming about money. The walls of the
penitentiary closed around us, and she raves alone, now,
in Charenton. I was saved, to paint again. My fellow
Americans brought me home, to paint upon the walls of
their cathedral. Paint! they said. Believe! they said. I
did. And I will finish it. My liver is on the way out, my
kidneys feel like balloons, but I will finish it. "Let us
rejoice in art, in our true faith!" my wife and I said to
each other. "Let us give ourselves up to the country of
our faith, and believe! We will be faithful! We believe!" *There.* Right there, Daughters of the Revolution, when the Judgment of Almighty God turns
against you and against your faith and against every-

thing you believe and hold dear, there it is: the Last Judgment. That's what I would paint across the walls of our church, on the faces of the damned, if I could. Someone will, some day. [*He weeps.*] Thank God for painting!

[*He lurches off. Enter* ESTHER *and* STRONG]

ESTHER: All right, George! Is religion true?

STRONG: Good God, Esther! I'm not going to answer that. I can tell you all about the bones of a caveman, but the bones of a saint—well, no. Ask me something easier. Ask me if science is true.

ESTHER: All right. Is science true?

STRONG: No.

ESTHER: What?

STRONG: It isn't true.

ESTHER: Then why do you say it is?

STRONG: I don't.

ESTHER: Then why do you spend your life running around in caves and rock quarries chasing fossils?

STRONG: To make it truer. Esther, it's a mystery either way. Don't you think you have to believe blindly in science, sometimes? Have faith? Submit? All that.

ESTHER: George, I can tell you I think your silly old fossils are a waste of time, and that's all right, but I couldn't say that to Stephen about the Christian church. Oh, George. Don't make me lose faith in you, too. You've always been so good to me. You're my big bug.

185

I trust you. Now I need to know what you really and truly think and you won't tell me.

STRONG: I'm destroyed. What do you want to know?

ESTHER: What do you think about religion?

STRONG: I think about it as little as possible.

ESTHER: George!

STRONG: I beg your pardon. Try it again.

ESTHER: Do you believe in God?

STRONG: No.

ESTHER: In a life after death? In a reward, a punishment? Seeing ever again those we love?

STRONG: Nursery tales.

ESTHER: You believe in nothing, then?

STRONG: Nothing but time. I am a geologist. I have seen time at work and I know it's there. But that's all.

ESTHER: That's horrible.

STRONG: What of it? I never said my faith was pleasant.

ESTHER: But then human life is nothing. Absolutely nothing.

STRONG: It is a part of time.

ESTHER: And that's all? My father, my life? Children, hands? Cameras, sacrifice, paint, glory, apple trees, love? Nothing but time?

STRONG: Nothing but time.

ESTHER: I don't want to believe that, George!

STRONG: Then marry Hazard! What's the trouble? He's raring to go! He'll give you everything you really want: God, immortal life, babies, the whole thing!

ESTHER: And church every Sunday! I don't want that, either!

STRONG: Esther!

ESTHER: I know! I'm impossible. But I'm trying! I want to believe in it all! I can! I will!

STRONG: Oh, stop it. You can't force yourself into faith. The thing is a state of mind, like jealousy.

ESTHER: Well, how do I get into that? Roll on the floor? See visions of devils and saints, and drink whiskey, like John Carrington? How do I catch the disease? What do I do?

STRONG: If you want Stephen—

ESTHER: I do!

STRONG: And you believe in him—

ESTHER: I do! I do!

STRONG: Then believe in his church! Why not? I don't see the problem!

ESTHER: I know you don't. Good old George.

STRONG: Esther, faith in anything is first of all submission. Religion, science, what have you. If you believe in your husband, then accept his work, his faith, his church. Submit!

ESTHER: Oh, George, you muttonhead! Don't you think I want to? Of course I do! I'd like to crawl after him in sackcloth and ashes! But I can't! I simply cannot!

187

STRONG [*taking her by the shoulders*]: Esther, Esther! You call everybody's bluff.

ESTHER: Really? That's what I do, is it?

STRONG: Yes, that's what you do.

ESTHER: Oh, George!

STRONG: Yes, my darling girl?

ESTHER: What in hell am I going to do?

[*She puts her arms around his neck and he holds her. Enter* HAZARD]

HAZARD: The laying on of hands, I assume. I didn't know your creed was that formal, George.

STRONG: Well, things evolve, Stephen. Look, I'm sorry.

HAZARD: Of course you are. I would be, too, if I were you.

ESTHER: George, I can't talk to him now. Make him go away. Stephen, go away!

HAZARD: No.

ESTHER: George, help!

STRONG: Well, Esther, what are you scared of? Tell him whatever you have to tell him. Just don't *you* be unhappy about it afterward.

ESTHER: George, you dunce! Of course I'll be unhappy about it afterward! I'm not a fossil, or a lump of coal!

STRONG: I know you're not!

ESTHER: He's a marvelous man!

STRONG: I know that! That's what I've been trying to tell you!

HAZARD: I'm sorry to butt in, but I resent being discussed in the third person while I stand here with my heart hanging out of my chest. George, if you please, sir.

STRONG: Shall I go, Esther?

ESTHER: Yes, you have to. But not far. And come right back!

STRONG: All right. Now, Stephen—

HAZARD: Go, George. Sin no more.

STRONG: Oh, boy. [*He stalks out.*]

ESTHER: This should never have happened. I was going to write to you. I'm going away.

HAZARD: No, no, Esther.

ESTHER: What?

HAZARD: I said, no, no. It won't do.

ESTHER: What won't do?

HAZARD: This exquisite tragedy, and grand rejection. I won't have it. You and I are going to get married as soon as we can and live a decent, happy, productive American life. Lots of work, lots of church, and lots of babies.

ESTHER: Is that so?

HAZARD: Yes, ma'am, it is! You can't leave me any more than I can leave you. Try it. Join the Moslems. Sail to China. You'll stand all night on the deck wanting me, and cut open the sheik's tent to let me in. I won't let you go!

ESTHER: Then you'll suffer for it!

189

HAZARD: Well, that's marriage, Esther, and we just have to do the best we can.

ESTHER: Stephen!

HAZARD: Well, what do you expect? Of course I'll suffer. I'll get hurt, and so will you. Tattered and torn. But if you run away, from me and from life, will you be torn any the less? I'm sorry to be dramatic, but you're the only woman I've ever loved, and I'll be damned if I'll let you go!

ESTHER: You'll save me, you mean?

HAZARD: Look at me, Esther! I was a man before I became a priest. Forget the priest and take the man, and in a year they won't be able to *keep* you out of church. You'll knock down the doors!

ESTHER: Stephen, I'm serious!

HAZARD: Hell, so am I! If you can tell me that you don't really love me, that you don't want me and desire me just as much as I want you and desire you, then good-by, preacher! Well, what do you say, tragedienne?

[ESTHER *throws herself into his arms. Conflagration, and a tangle of arms and mouths*]

ESTHER [*hugging and kissing*]: Oh, God, you're merciless! Merciless!

HAZARD [*hugging and kissing*]: I'm in love, damn it all! And so are you!

ESTHER [*hugging and kissing*]: I know it! You're right! You're right!

HAZARD [*hugging and kissing*]: Of course I am! We're in love!

ESTHER: Well, all right, then! If my love is what you want then take it! I'll lie down in your arms this minute! [*She kisses him fiercely.*] And ruin your life with such pleasure!

[*She is quite wild.* HAZARD *holds her, but now to calm her down. Sure of his victory, he laughs.*]

HAZARD: Ruined lives, indeed! Why do you worry about that petty parish gossip? All that will stop the instant we are married. Good Lord, if I didn't sometimes shock my parish, how do you think I could manage it?

[*Pause. Long pause. In his arms,* ESTHER *stiffens slightly, and detaches herself, gently.*]

ESTHER: I see. [*She steps back, breathing deeply, and stares at him with deep bewilderment.*] But I would rather not be used for that purpose. Or myself managed, like that.

HAZARD [*reaching for her*]: Oh, I was joking!

ESTHER: No. [*She steps back.*] Let me catch my breath.

HAZARD: I was *joking!*

ESTHER: I wasn't. And that's the way it still is with us. After the beautiful storm rides by, I mean. Stephen, let's tell each other the truth.

HAZARD: We have! We do!

ESTHER: No. We don't. We're such liars, we can't even tell when we're fibbing and when we aren't. But let's try now. Please.

HAZARD: All right. Go ahead.

ESTHER: I want you so much I will believe anything to get you. So I tell myself. It's a lie. It isn't true.

HAZARD: You don't have to worry—

ESTHER: But I do. I can't live with it, Stephen.

HAZARD: With what, for crying out loud?

ESTHER: American religion! Brute belief! When you want something, you *will* it to happen, force it to exist, by saying it is already so! Shut your eyes, believe hard enough, with enough power and force, never admit it can't happen, and it will!

HAZARD: Yes! That is what I call faith! Faith in life, in ourselves, in our country! It will bring us success and happiness.

ESTHER: That is what I call madness. Lunacy. It will bring us delusion and ruin.

HAZARD: Then what are you going to do, Esther? How else are you going to live?

ESTHER: By candor. Or at least by not becoming a common liar. My father—

HAZARD: Esther, let's not talk about your father right now, if you don't mind.

ESTHER: All right, let's talk about me. I'm not fit to be a clergyman's wife. I'd be a scandal in the church. Sooner or later you would choose between it and me. I wouldn't stand a chance.

HAZARD: How do you know that?

ESTHER: I know that some people are not made to trust in the promised land. You are. I'm not. I'm afraid! I live in fear!

HAZARD: Fear?

ESTHER: Yes. Don't you know what that means?

HAZARD: My darling girl, do you think that I, whose hands are always raw from the grasp of men and women in their death agonies, who sees every day the power of my faith, do you think I am frightened by your common, daily, matter-of-fact fears and doubts? I have them myself. In the face of pain, and age, and eternity, they go away.

ESTHER: I'm sorry but that's not true. If your fears and doubts were as strong as mine, you wouldn't be a priest.

HAZARD: Do you think that I don't bury and baptize and pray for the dead in fear and doubt? Of course I do. The priest doesn't exist who hasn't. But must that cost me my faith? Human life is impossible without faith in something, and it's *life*, Esther, that I want to give you!

ESTHER: And to give me life, you will have me stand up in that church every Sunday and say I believe in things that I don't? And neither do you? Say *yes* when we mean *no*, and *I will* when we mean *I won't?* What kind of life is that?

HAZARD: The only kind there is. The life to which we are born, and must live. Religion is stark reality, Esther. You have to come to terms with it, like a peasant with his king, or a citizen with his government.

ESTHER: But I can't, my dear. I won't. I refuse.

HAZARD: I see. [*Pause*] Well, tell me, then: What are these terrible fears and doubts? Drag them out.

ESTHER: Stephen, don't.

HAZARD: Well, am I just to walk away, then, because of a few morbid fancies? Esther!

ESTHER: All right. You want to know why I run away from you and I will tell you. I hate the church. I do not simply dislike it, I despise it. To sit in that body of abject, carnivorous, dishonest American hypocrites revolts me. And you. I never see you conduct the service without feeling you are some priest in a dim pagan temple. I half expect you to bring out a goat or a ram, slice open its throat on the high altar, and throw its blood on me. Shall I, with such ideas as that, join you in Christ's holy communion?

HAZARD [*stung*]: What you call pagan is to me the mystery of tradition. It is more real to me than chemistry. But a ceremony needn't stand in your way. The church is broad enough and sure enough to allow you to disregard ceremonies, and to feel the eternal truths behind them.

ESTHER: And what are they? The ceremonies are at least picturesque, and I could get used to them, but the truths behind them are more pagan than the ceremonies! You see? I've hurt you enough. Let me go.

HAZARD: No.

ESTHER: All right.

HAZARD: Every church, every faith, is subject to attack. I won't contest that, or the deep pleasures of saying no. But don't you tremble at what lies ahead of you? Are you more than human? Can you really face life, death, and eternity alone? With no communion of the spirit? No fellowship of flesh and blood?

ESTHER: But your church is all blood and flesh, and no spirit at all! You cry flesh! flesh! flesh! from every altar in that cathedral!

HAZARD: Don't degrade the church, Esther. The church satisfied God's holy saints. It was good enough for them.

ESTHER: But it is not good enough for me! It must be we are living in a different world now, for I see nothing spiritual about the church. It is a maze of deceit, from the door to the altar!

HAZARD: Esther! How can you possibly say that?

[ESTHER *turns on him. Her blood is up, and father's fierceness blazes within her.*]

ESTHER: Then do you really believe in the resurrection of the flesh?

HAZARD [*after a second*]: Yes! Yes, of course, I do!

ESTHER: Then why can't you look at me when you say so?

HAZARD: I can! I do!

ESTHER: Then I do not believe *you*. Or perhaps you can't even tell the difference between what is true and what is only necessary to believe. Resurrection of the flesh, indeed. To me that is the most shocking and immoral of all human ideas. It must be so to you. It is a bribe, paid by liars to seduce the hopeless. Am I to have you make me believe that I will see my father's flesh again? That he will give me again the love that fed my childhood and hold me again in those strong arms I know lie rotting in the earth? That is obscene! You throw flesh and self at me from every corner of your church.

195

I don't want to find myself, I want to give it away. But you will pursue me with myself down into my grave, and stamp it upon me there in the dust!

HAZARD [*angry*]: Do you think any of this is new? I have heard all these wretched arguments since I was a schoolboy. I won't argue over trifles! One question, Esther. That's all. Answer against me, and I'll go away and never bother you again.

ESTHER: Oh, Stephen!

HAZARD: Resurrection shocks you, does it? Then tell me this: Can you, without being shocked a great deal worse, imagine any life, past, present, or future, without those for whom God created you: without your father, without your husband, and, as you are a woman, without your child?

ESTHER: Oh, that is the worst! That is rock bottom! That is vile, and filthy! I ask you for spiritual life again and what do you do again? Again you send me back into myself, back into my flesh and my blood, this time back into my own womb, like a bitch to her puppies! Are you such a coward, that you use a woman's sex against her?

HAZARD [*finally exploding*]: Oh, coward, my foot! You're a fraud, Esther Dudley!

ESTHER: What?

HAZARD: You're not running away from me because you hate the church or love your impossible morality, but because you can't bear the thought of living with any other man but your father! And you never will! Nobody will ever be good enough for you but him! You wanted the truth, my dear? All right! *There it is!*

ESTHER: And there *you* are, ready to kill me with it! If that is finally and really the truth, Reverend Stephen Hazard, then tell me this: Why is it my fault that he was a better man than you?

[STRONG *enters.*]

STRONG: You can be heard all over town. Sorry.

HAZARD: You started this. Why?

STRONG: If I did, I didn't mean to.

ESTHER: But he didn't. Did he, Stephen?

HAZARD: No, I guess not. Good-by, Esther. I won't trouble you again, unless, again, you need me, as you once did. If you do, I will be there, and so will the church, to do our best. Good-by. God bless you. [*He leaves.*]

STRONG: Esther, I think you're wonderful.

ESTHER: But George, I don't love you. I love him.

[*They part. Enter, with vigor,* RAITCLIFFE *and* MRS. LEE]

MRS. LEE: I'm sure you would rather I speak quickly and frankly. I couldn't answer you when you did me the honor of proposing marriage, but I can now. It's impossible. Let's return to our early friendship, which I enjoyed so much.

RAITCLIFFE: May I ask why?

MRS. LEE: Of course. The truth is, I did wonder if my life might not be best spent in helping you, as your wife.

But our lives run on different tracks, and we are both too old to change.

RAITCLIFFE [*smiling*]: Your reasoning is not very sound. We fit together hand and glove. I can give you excitement, vitality, and real opportunity. While you can give my life the love and grace for which it is starved. If that's your only argument, I'm sure I can resolve it to your satisfaction.

MRS. LEE: I won't argue with you. We simply have different views of life. I can't accept yours. You would be smothered to death by mine.

RAITCLIFFE: Show me! Show me one single example of such a difference, and I will accept your decision without another word.

MRS. LEE: Do you insist?

RAITCLIFFE [*quietly*]: I believe I do.

MRS. LEE: Very well.

[*She hands him the letter given her by* CARRINGTON. *He glances at it very briefly indeed and calmly hands it back, indifferently. She then tears it into pieces and puts them into an ashtray.*]

RAITCLIFFE: I would have told you about that myself.

MRS. LEE: Would you? Then it is true you wrote that letter?

RAITCLIFFE: Well, my dear Madeleine, of course it's true. What of it? I wrote that letter, yes, with this hand, quite so. But for whom did I do it, will you consider that?

MRS. LEE: I would rather not.

RAITCLIFFE: You will just walk away from me then? From a man who has come to love you deeply, and whose progress into devotion you did not exactly impede. Now surely you will hear me out.

MRS. LEE: You are quite right. Please go ahead.

RAITCLIFFE: Thank you. Lincoln almost lost his election —did you know that? Well, he did. The party believed that if he lost, the country was lost. Money was freely spent and freely borrowed. We won. Well and good. But loans, my dear, must be repaid. I was asked by the party to abandon my opposition to a certain steamship subsidy. I did not ask why. It was essential to the interests of the party. I voted for the subsidy. It passed, by a majority. Everything ran smoothly.

MRS. LEE [*acidly*]: And how much did they pay you?

RAITCLIFFE [*indignant*]: They paid the Republican party one hundred thousand dollars, madam, which elected to the Presidency, Abraham Lincoln, *who saved the Union!* And for that money, in due course, the party paid that company back with a subsidy to run its ships.

MRS. LEE: And you simply stood there, handing the money from one batch of thieves to another? None of it stuck?

RAITCLIFFE: Even if you think I'm dishonest, do you think I'm a fool? The money was paid to the party. I didn't take a penny.

MRS. LEE: Quote: "My handling of this affair has saved your company and our interests over twelve thousand dollars," unquote. Am I to believe you wrote that in the interests of statistical accuracy? Or didn't you play the company against the party and the party against the company, with that vote of yours, and then get yourself paid twelve thousand dollars for it? No wonder you are highly thought of in Washington!

RAITCLIFFE: All right. It is the public act of my life I most regret. Not for the doing of it, but for the necessity of doing it, since the party insisted. I deplore it just as you do. There is still no real difference between us.

MRS. LEE [*icily*]: I am afraid I cannot agree with you.

RAITCLIFFE: Oh, why can't you understand the obvious? It seems to me you are from another planet, you are so ignorant of plain American reality. Life hands us conflicting duties. In all but the simplest things, we find ourselves obligated to violate some moral tenet, some abstract notion of the right and the true, and the pure. We have to do it, whether we like it or not, and we do! And thank God we do! Otherwise this country would break in pieces!

MRS. LEE: Would it? Are you so sure of that?

RAITCLIFFE: Yes, I'm sure! I am a servant of the United States! I have obligations and duties which will not allow me the perfections of a self-righteous schoolboy! But of course I could be like that. With my little volume of Plato or Voltaire under my arm, I could say perish the government, perish the Union, perish the people themselves, rather than I soil these white hands or blemish this perfect conscience. But I do not say that. I say, be my fate what it will, this glorious Union, the last hope of all suffering humanity, shall be preserved! Whatever the cost, whatever the sacrifice, so help me God!

MRS. LEE: And twelve thousand dollars. You are a moral lunatic.

[*He stares at her, astonished, and she, astonished, at him.*]

RAITCLIFFE: That is a terrible thing to say to me! Have I ever hidden my beliefs on this subject? Have I ever pretended to be above the difficulties of practical life? I have not. Didn't I even tell you—of my own free will —of an act far worse than the writing of that miserable letter? And didn't you nod your head, and say, "Yes, yes, of course"? My dear woman, in Illinois, I violated the sanctity of a great popular election! I reversed its results! I deprived one million people of their votes under the Constitution of the United States! I took from them rights that belong to them as absolutely as their houses, for which they have shed their blood. And did you say I was wrong then? You did not. Did you say I was dishonest? You did not. By your silence, you ratify my action just as if you perform it yourself. Why are you so self-righteous about a smaller crime, when you have already approved a larger one?

MRS. LEE: Secretary Raitcliffe, I am trying to refuse, as graciously as possible, your proposal of marriage, not attack or blame you in any way. I'm certain you do what you think is right, according to a code in which you deeply believe. But finally, I do not believe in it! I can't live with it! Don't press me any further!

RAITCLIFFE: But I *must* press you further! You are my future! I need your help. There's nothing I won't do to get it. Do you require affection? I am filled with it. My concern for you is boundless. Do you doubt that, Madeleine?

MRS. LEE: No, no.

RAITCLIFFE: Are you afraid of being dragged into the mire of ordinary political life? I will never let that happen to us. My greatest wish is to have your help in purifying politics, in reducing the corruption we have so often discussed. What higher ambition could you want?

MRS. LEE: If I have learned anything at all, it is that I could do nothing sillier than suppose myself competent to reform anything in Washington. That's absurd, and you know it. It is only bait that you dangle before me, like a nest of worms impaled on steel hooks. Allow me to refuse, and swim away. I no longer cling to my life. I do not even value it very highly, but I cannot utterly disgrace it.

RAITCLIFFE: And what, for God's sake, does that mean?

MRS. LEE: That means I will not share stolen goods! I will not turn moral somersaults, and every day of my life maintain that immorality is virtue!

RAITCLIFFE: I had hoped to find a courage in you that would disregard much risk. If everyone talked like you, the country would soon perish. Don't put yourself up on a column, like a saint in the desert. You'll wither away. I plead your cause as I plead mine. Don't sacrifice your life, the life of a beautiful, vibrant, useful, woman!

MRS. LEE: Rather more useful than beautiful or vibrant, I believe. I won't discuss it further.

DEMOCRACY AND ESTHER

[RAITCLIFFE *clenches his hands and breathes deeply. He is a very tenacious man.*]

RAITCLIFFE: But is there no vow I make to you? No pledge? No sacrifice? You dislike politics, now. Very well. Shall I leave political life?

MRS. LEE: What did you say?

RAITCLIFFE: I love you. Do you believe me now?

MRS. LEE: Why—why—

RAITCLIFFE: Let's see! I could certainly ask for the post of British minister! You would have four years in London, with no politics. Your social position there would be the best in the world. Four years is not forever!

MRS. LEE: And we could take that chance at the White House just as well as this one! But we won't!

RAITCLIFFE [*desperate*]: Ah, Madeleine! I can't live without you! The sound of your voice! The touch of your hand! The rustle of your dress! They are like wine to me! For God's sake, don't refuse me now!

[*He grabs her hand and presses himself against her. She moves away.*]

MRS. LEE: I will not be bought by cheap theatre any more than by a British ministry. No bribe will change my life. Let's have no more of this.

RAITCLIFFE: What do you mean, no more of it? You talk like we're some damn little boy and girl in a canoe! Hell, fire! That's my life's blood you're spilling all over the ground! I'm in trouble, Queen of Sheba! It's expected we get married! Now, I didn't come running after you; you came running after me! You knew what you wanted, and now, by God, you have got it! Marry me, Madeleine! *I have got to have it, and you are going to give it to me!*

[*And in a moment, she does. Slowly, deliberately, and accurately, she slaps him full in the face. Then, just as slowly, she turns and sweeps out of the room.* RAIT-CLIFFE *is left bursting, choking with rage. Enter* JACOBI, *with hat, white gloves, orchid, and cane. He sees* RAITCLIFFE *in obvious frustration. He holds his orchid out to* RAITCLIFFE *with polite malice.*]

JACOBI: My congratulations?

[RAITCLIFFE *thrusts him roughly out of the way.*]

RAITCLIFFE: Ah, you God-damned little pansy!

JACOBI: Raitcliffe!

RAITCLIFFE [*whirling about*]: Sir?

[JACOBI, *his moment come, lifts his white gloves and strikes* RAITCLIFFE *across the face, and* RAITCLIFFE *gets it again. He roars, lifts both arms in fury. Then, realizing what might happen if he attacked the old man, bellows with a horrible passion and rushes out.* JACOBI *smiles, shrugs, turns to the front.*]

JACOBI: And that, as I promised to show you, was the end of Jacobi, Bulgarian Minister, and his Thirty Years in Washington. [*He moves downstage, in a spotlight. The rest of the stage darkens.*] It isn't fatal. There's a small bank in Switzerland to buy me orchids, and see me politely to the grave. And I adore Europe by steamship. The sea gives one a feeling of liberation, if the company is good. This year, it is choice.

[*He holds out his arms. From the darkness come* ESTHER *and* MRS. LEE, *in traveling clothes. He kisses their hands and smiles.*]

A wicked old man could hardly do better.

[*He moves away, leaving the two women standing alone on the stage. A steam whistle blows. Above them, a light brightens on* HAZARD *and* STRONG, *who have come to see them off.*]

HAZARD: Well, George, what do we say? You know, she reminded me of some trim little yacht you might come upon, all alone in mid-ocean. Sailing along, no land in sight, with great waves and cold winds rising up to crush her. What can you do but wonder what on earth she was doing, out there?

STRONG: Well, Stephen, I say this. In this morning's paper, I see the latest scandal broke, and the Boss said, "Nothing is lost, boys, but honor." Well, there go Esther Dudley and Madeleine Lee, and nothing is lost, my friend, but beauty.

[*A burst of music from a marching band. Another light brightens on* CANDIDATE SILAS RAITCLIFFE *and on his wife, who stands with him,* ESSY BAKER RAITCLIFFE. *They wave.*]

CANDIDATE RAITCLIFFE: Ladies and gentlemen, we're right here with you to celebrate our nomination and to promise you a victory in the fall! We hope you all have a pleasant time here today! I mean to, and so does Essy.

ESSY BAKER RAITCLIFFE: I certainly do!

[*Everyone in the play comes to* RAITCLIFFE *and* ESSY

and start shaking hands, as with GRANT *earlier. Everyone but the two beautiful women, of course, who stand isolated from their country and their people, moving away. The whistle blows.*]

MRS. LEE: And do you know, Esther, the most bitter thing in this whole comedy?

ESTHER: No, what?

MRS. LEE: Nine out of ten of our fellow countrymen will tell us we have made a mistake!

[*Farewell and darkness, and the jaunty, hopeful music of the American marching band.*]